D0684243

pocket posh® word power

120 JOB INTERVIEW WORDS
YOU SHOULD KNOW

pocket posh® word power

120 JOB INTERVIEW WORDS
YOU SHOULD KNOW

w♥rdnik®

**Andrews McMeel
Publishing, LLC**

Kansas City • Sydney • London

Copyright © 2011 by Wordnik®. All rights reserved. Printed
in China. No part of this book may be used or reproduced
in any manner whatsoever without written permission
except in the case of reprints in the context of reviews.

Andrews McMeel Publishing, LLC
an Andrews McMeel Universal company
1130 Walnut Street, Kansas City, Missouri 64106

www.andrewsmcmeel.com

11 12 13 14 15 LEO 10 9 8 7 6 5 4 3 2 1

ISBN: 978-1-4494-0138-2

Library of Congress Control Number: 2010934821

Project Editor: Angela Tung

Illustration by Heather Bailey

ATTENTION: SCHOOLS AND BUSINESSES
Andrews McMeel books are available at quantity discounts
with bulk purchase for educational, business, or sales
promotional use. For information, please e-mail the
Andrews McMeel Publishing Special Sales Department:
specialsales@amuniversal.com

preface

A job interview is a very stressful situation: You only have a few minutes to make that crucial first impression, and you must do it while wearing uncomfortable clothes, in an unfamiliar place, and with someone you may never have met before.

The secret to making that essential, crucial first impression is being prepared, and one way to be prepared is to have at your command knowledge of today's business buzzwords—not necessarily to use them, but to be able to acknowledge their use and to get past them to the real substance of the matter.

The interviewer may toss around words like agile and adhocracy, but what he or she is really asking is, "Are you a flexible and creative person, or are you hidebound and overly dependent on set processes?" Similarly, questions about bandwidth and throughput are not inquiries about your technical knowledge, but rather about your ability to set good priorities and achieve quick results.

Some of these words (especially verbs ending in –ize) are often frowned upon as being "too jargony." It's best to wait for your interviewer to be the first to use these words.

Good luck!

1

aboveboard

/ (ə-buv'bôrd͵ *or* ə-buv'bōrd͵)/

adjective

- In open sight; without tricks or disguise: as, an honest man deals *aboveboard*; his actions are open and *aboveboard*.

Examples:

In the latter category, an e-mail exchange between two Morgan Stanley employees discusses a client who seems to want to step around the terms of a contract signed with a third party. A Morgan Stanley employee advises telling the company to stay "*aboveboard*" and follow the letter of the contract. —Kim Zetter, "BlackBerry Reveals Bank's Secrets," *Wired*, August 25, 2003

Senator Strom Thurmond of South Carolina came to national prominence when he stormed out of the 1948 Democratic National Convention after the party endorsed civil rights for African-Americans. . . . Racial segregation, he added, was red-white-and-blue American, for it was "honest, open and *aboveboard*." —Geoffrey R. Stone, "The Wrong Side of History," *The Huffington Post*, June 10, 2007

Aboveboard was originally a term in gambling: A gambler whose hands were "above the board" or table could not cheat by changing cards below the table.

accountability

/ (ə-koun'tə-bil'i-tē)/

noun

- The state of being accountable or answerable; responsibility for the fulfillment of obligations; liability to account for conduct, meet or suffer consequences, and so on.

Examples:

Tough talk on teacher accountability is all the rage this summer. Trouble is, we don't know how to handle the perverse incentives that arise the moment we place undue weight on easily manipulated exams. But that hasn't stopped a slew of education leaders from weighing in on the need to hold teachers' feet to the fire. —Justin Snider, "Why you should be skeptical about standardized test scores," *The Washington Post*, August 7, 2010

However, with the No Child Left Behind reauthorization debate underway, the definition of that unassailable word, "accountability," is under attack by interests with an eye for pumping up statistics rather than students' actual learning. —Dan Brown, "The School Accountability Trap," *The Huffington Post*, September 20, 2007

Accountability also has the military definition of "the obligation imposed by law or lawful order or regulation on an officer or other person for keeping accurate record of property, documents, or funds."

3   acquisition

/ (ak,wi-zish'ən)/

noun

1 The act of acquiring or gaining possession, as the *acquisition* of property.

2 That which is acquired or gained, especially a company that is purchased by another company.

Examples:

For P&G, the Cincinnati-based maker of household brands including Pampers diapers, Gillette razors and Dawn dish soap, the acquisition [of Nioxin Research Inc., a family-run, closely held maker of products to address thinning hair] is the latest step in an aggressive march into the beauty market. —Elly Byron, "Procter & Gamble Acquires Maker of Thinning-Hair Products," *The Wall Street Journal*, September 4, 2008

Under the acquisition, which has been in the works for several months, former Senate majority leader Trent Lott (R-Miss.) and former senator John Breaux (D-La.) will join Patton Boggs [Washington's biggest lobbying firm] along with their sons, Chester Trent Lott and John Breaux Jr., and a half-dozen other staff members, according to a news release. —Dan Eggen, "Patton Boggs lobbying firm buys group run by Lott, Breaux," *The Washington Post*, July 2, 2010

Mergers and acquisitions often go hand in hand. A merger is "the legal union of two or more corporations into a single entity, with assets and liabilities typically being assumed by the buying party."

4

action item

/ (ak'shən ī'təm)/

noun

- A task; especially an item discussed in a meeting that requires further action or work.

Examples:

School district taxpayers would have to vote on creating a Fund 80 at the annual meeting on Monday, Aug. 23. The meeting agenda includes the issue as an action item, though it is unclear what action the board will take. —Gina Duwe, "Evansville Youth Center's funding source could change," *Gazette Xtra*, August 7, 2010

Marshall said that the issue of passing Sun Tran off to the RTA will be the top action item at Wednesday's City Council meeting. —"The complexities of the Sun Tran strike: Tucson vs RTA," *Tucson Citizen*, August 6, 2010

Some of the recommendations in this and other sections are breathtaking in their scope, while others are very specific. In the "Natural Legacy" section, for example, one action item is "implement initiatives that conserve the Maine Woods at a scale large enough to protect the integrity of the forest ecosystem," while another specifically asks "improve eelgrass monitoring in order to develop healthier eelgrass beds." —George Smith, "A Path to Economic and Environmental Happiness," *Down East*, July 20, 2010

Ironically, often we have found that what is missing is an easy action item for the consumer. —Laura Noonan, "Advertising Campaigns Are Not Etched in Stone," *Dealer Marketing Magazine*, August 3, 2010

Several *action items* might make up an *action plan*.

(5) **adhocracy**
/ (ad hok', hōk' rə-sē)/

noun

- An organizational system designed to be flexible and responsive to the needs of the moment rather than excessively bureaucratic, or ruled by structure and regulations.

Examples:
He'd only hesitated for a second when Andrew asked him to be the inaugural advisor on ParasiteNet's board, and once he'd said yes, it became clear to everyone that he was endlessly fascinated by their little adhocracy and its experimen-

tal telco potential. —Cory Doctorow, *Someone Comes to Town, Someone Leaves Town*, 2005

The "miracle" of the Obama campaign, Carr believes, was how it "organized itself," through an "adhocracy self-assigned by geography and expertise." —"Politics and Popular Culture," *MIT World*, February 26, 2009

He said that adhocracy, according to academics, is an organization which is the opposite of a bureaucracy. One that cuts across bureaucratic lines to capture opportunities, solve problems, and get results. —Mike Carlton, "Is Your Agency an Adhocracy?" *Knol*, May 2009

Adhocracy was formed by combining the Latin phrase *ad hoc*, meaning "created on the spur of the moment," with the suffix *-cracy*, which comes from the Greek word *kratiā*, meaning "rule, strength."

(6) **aggregator**
/ (ag'rigā̠tər)/

noun

- Someone or something that aggregates, especially a business that collects the output of many other businesses or sources.

Examples:

That's why there's growing interest in packaging small parcels of forestland into carbon portfolios that can then be traded competitively on voluntary markets. Woodlands Carbon Company, an Oregon-based pilot project funded by the American Forest Foundation, is just one so-called aggregator looking to pool the carbon trading power of forest owners. —Jessica Knoblauch, "Pacific NW landowners team up to market forest offsets," *Grist*, August 11, 2009

The beauty of an aggregator is that it displays articles from hundreds of websites in one place, so the user doesn't have to pull up the sites individually. —Ryan Singel, "Will RSS Readers Clog the Web?" *Wired*, April 30, 2004

Some Web sites allow travelers to compare insurance policies from several companies at once. Two of the main aggregator sites, according to people contacted by CNN, are Squaremouth.com and InsureMyTrip.com. —John D. Sutter, "Nervous Travelers Demanding 'Layoff Insurance,'" *CNN*, March 5, 2009

In short, an aggregator is a site that summarizes content that lives on other sites. —Danny Sullivan, "He Calls Google a Vampire, But Mark Cuban's Mahalo Is Doing the Sucking," *Search Engine Land*, February 3, 2010

An *aggregator* can also be an online feed reader used to keep track of updates to blogs, news sources, and other Web sites.

agile

/ (aj'əl *or* aj'īl͵)/

adjective

1 Responding quickly to customer needs or market changes; not tied to previous business practices.
2 In computing, *agile development* is an iterative and collaborative approach to software development done by flexible teams that take into account rapidly changing conditions in the market.

Examples:

Agile companies have what athletes and soldiers call "situational awareness." They put themselves both in a position to observe what's happening and have the wherewithal to act upon that intelligence. —Faisal Hoque, "How to Bring Agility Into the Business," *CIO Update*, August 11, 2010

While many Chinese companies are agile and have lofty ambitions, some of them lack the efficient management systems and processes needed to implement their goals. China's imperfect institutional environment and rapidly changing marketplace entice many domestic companies to rush to take advantage of "opportunities" without careful analysis. —Zhu Xiaoming and Pedro Nueno, "Ventures Abroad Facing a Bumpy Road," *China Daily*, September 6, 2010

I would like to have explained to him that in agile development, one of the objectives is to surface as many "mistakes" and "unproductive paths" as early in the process as possible. This generates a lot of learning, and makes the productive paths more visible. —Mike Bonifer, "Solar the Sign!" *The Huffington Post*, April 24, 2009

Agile comes from the Latin word agere, meaning "to drive, do."

8

alignment

/ (ə-līn'mənt)/

noun

- The act of organizing groups into agreement, especially around a shared goal or belief, or the state of being in agreement.

Examples:

Unless every aspect of your business presence is in alignment with your values-based environmental proposition, the results will not follow the effort. —Josh Dorfman, "Your Company's Green Credibility: Everything Is Communicating Something," *The Huffington Post*, May 16, 2010

While Focus on the Family is pleased the American Psychological Association reaffirmed its position that clients have a right to pursue sexual orientation change in alignment with their religious faith, Mr. Myers wrongly implies that Focus only recently concluded sexual orientation is not a "choice." —Melissa Fryrear, "Focus on the Family Recipes," *The Wall Street Journal*, September 2, 2009

The vice president asked that his teams make sure that their goals were in alignment with their customers' needs. —Wordnik

The business sense of *alignment* is related to the military sense of having all the members of a squadron or platoon in the correct places before the start of a battle.

9   **anonymize**
/ (ə-nän'ə-mīz͵)/

verb

 * To make anonymous; to remove identifying personal information.

Examples:
A key component of ThinThread was privacy protection. The program could collect domestic data but would "anonymize" names and other identifying information with

10

encryption codes until evidence was gathered to justify a warrant so that names could be revealed. —Ellen Nakashima, "Former NSA executive Thomas A. Drake may pay high price for media leak," *The Washington Post*, July 14, 2010

PatientsLikeMe allows people with chronic diseases to create public profiles listing their symptoms, medications, and other details long deemed too sensitive to share. . . . The company, meanwhile, anonymizes the data and sells it to medical researchers and drug developers. —Brendan I. Koerner, "Jamie Heywood: Forget Medical Privacy," *Wired*, September 21, 2009

Anonymize is an example of *anthimeria*, turning a word from one part of speech into another, in this case from an adjective, *anonymous*, into a verb.

10

bailout
/ (bāl'out̩) /

noun
  • A rescue, especially a financial rescue.

Examples:
But in the long term the bailout is actually not a good thing, in my view. I'd much rather see Mexico achieve credibility on its own by taking real steps toward reform. They need to show that they're going to cut spending, privatize more

companies and do a better job of naming the government.
—"Spanning the Globe," *Newsweek*, February 13, 1995

And if a total taxpayer bailout is the real plan, it would be far better to do it straightforwardly with something like a Reconstruction Finance Corporation. A new RFC would conduct real audits of troubled banks (not "stress tests"), determine how much capital they needed, and decide what combination of taxpayer and Federal Reserve assistance, coupled with sacrifices from bondholders and shareholders, would make up the gap. —Robert Kuttner, "Obama's Loyal Opposition," *The Huffington Post*, April 13, 2009

A final irony: In the credit crisis, the one class of financial-services firm that has not collapsed or begged for a bailout is the hedge-fund industry. —L. Gordon Crovitzthe, "Don't Sell Short Sellers Short," *The Wall Street Journal*, July 28, 2008

A *bailout* is also "a backup supply of air in scuba diving."

11 **ballpark**
/ (bôl′pärk₁)/

noun
1 The general vicinity; somewhere close; a broad approximation.

2 A field, stadium, or park where ball, especially baseball, is played.

adjective
- Approximate; close; on the right order of magnitude.

verb
- To make a rough estimate.

Examples:

He writes: "Pick up the mission statement of almost any college or university, and you will find claims and ambitions that will lead you to think that it is the job of an institution of higher learning to cure every ill the world has ever known: not only illiteracy and cultural ignorance, which are at least in the ballpark, but poverty, war, racism, gender bias . . . and the hegemony of Wal-Mart." —Naomi Schaefer Riley, "When Academic Freedom Lost Its Meaning," *The Wall Street Journal*, October 24, 2008

"Could you ballpark the cost for me?" asked Ron after the advertising agency presented their approach to his project. "Just give me an estimate." —Wordnik

As you might imagine, determining how the human brain works with functional magnetic resonance imaging (fMRI) is in the same ball-park of difficulty as determining how our mystery computer works with only a temperature sensor. — Dan Agin, "Neurobank: Politics, Phrenics, and Brainscans," *The Huffington Post*, November 11, 2007

The terms *ballpark estimate* or *ballpark figure* are often used in business. *Ballpark* is occasionally spelled *ball-park*.

12 **bandwidth**

/ (band'width, *or* band'with,)/

noun

1 A measure of data flow rate in digital networks typically in bits per second.

2 The capacity, energy, or time required to achieve a particular goal or complete a task.

Examples:

It's been interesting to watch the reaction to Google's announcement of open access Internet service to select American homes at a jaw-dropping 1 Gbps. That's roughly a 100-fold increase in bandwidth from the maximum speeds offered by most of the larger Internet service providers today. —Don Tapscott, "Google Raises the Bar," *The Huffington Post*, February 11, 2010

With bandwidth-intensive technologies, like streaming video or file uploads, the ability to asynchronously handle this data when the bandwidth is available, but also remain usable when the bandwidth is not available, is very exciting. —Michael Arrington, "Adobe Apollo Launched, So Go Build Something," *TechCrunch*, March 18, 2007

I do not normally cover these kinds of things and my bandwidth is a little taken up by mobile related stories but I will try to cover the basics. —Justin Oberman, "POST TC50: Politics4All Launches a New Political Social Networking Site," *Personal Democracy Forum*, September 15, 2008

"Do you have the *bandwidth*?" someone might ask you. They mean, "Do you have the time to get this done?"

(13) **bear market**
/ (bâr mär'kit)/

noun
- A stock market where a majority of investors are selling ("bears"), causing overall stock prices to drop.

Examples:
But those who've bought into Berkshire in the course of the past nineteen months have been served rather poorly, with little explanation as to why other than this has been a bear market and their shares have suffered as have most other

shareholders in most other funds and companies. —David Berman, "Gartman vs Buffett, round three," *The Globe and Mail*, June 24, 2009

When I asked Mr. Prechter if such valuations were realistic, he replied that earnings and dividends must fall drastically to parallel previous bear-market lows. —Jason Zweig, "Get Ready for a Cataclysmic Market Crash! (or Maybe Not)," *The Wall Street Journal*, July 10, 2010

The term *bear market* may have come from the proverb, "To sell the bear's skin before catching the bear," with the idea of selling stocks on speculation. Also *bear-market*, when used as an adjective.

14

benchmark
/ (bench'märk,)/

noun
- A standard by which something is evaluated or measured.

verb
- To measure the performance of an item relative to another similar item in an impartial scientific manner.

Examples:
Generally, small-cap funds are considered bloated when assets surpass $800 million; for mid-cap funds the benchmark is around $3 billion; and large-cap funds may be getting too

big at about $18 billion, Mr. Kinnel says. —Karen Hube, "Think Before Unloading," *The Wall Street Journal*, November 3, 2008

The choice of a benchmark is the "front line of defense against inflation, and also it's at the heart of the central bank being able to precisely and flexibly guide interest-rate policy in the recovery," said Goodfriend, now a professor at Carnegie Mellon University in Pittsburgh. —Scott Lanman, "Fed Weighs Interest on Reserves as New Benchmark Rate," *Bloomberg Business Week*, January 26, 2010

McClintic, also president of the Columbia Missouri National Education Association, acknowledged later that the benchmark is a cliché but said she asked about his early plans because it's a question journalists often ask presidents, and she saw a parallel. —Hayley Tsukayama, "Columbia Public Schools superintendent off to a brisk start," *Columbia Missourian*, October 20, 2009

Benchmark originally referred to a surveyor's mark made on some stationary object and shown on a map, used as a reference point.

15

best-of-breed
/ (best uv brēd)/

noun
- Any product thought to be the best of its type.

Examples:

For years CIOs have had to choose between best-of-breed applications that were focused on solving one problem and combined suites of many applications built to work together.
—Dan Woods, "Compliance in the Best-of-Breed Cloud," *Forbes*, July 20, 2010

In a research note, analyst David Magee wrote, "At a time when overall retail visibility is low, Bed Bath & Beyond is, in our view, a relatively safe haven . . . a best-of-breed operator with a strong balance sheet, and as evidenced by the second-quarter report, the ability to execute effectively even in the absence of an industry tailwind." —"Stocks in the Spotlight Thursday," *Barron's*, September 25, 2008

The Bush administration claimed Lotus Notes was antiquated and not up to the job. That is categorically incorrect. Lotus Notes is regularly updated and is an IBM flagship product. I have personally seen many extensive, enterprise-grade solutions with Notes that are absolutely best-of-breed.
—Joan Brunwasser, "Part Two of Interview with David Gewirtz, Author of *Where Have All the Emails Gone?*" *OpEdNews.com*, March 30, 2009

Best-of-breed comes from the title given at competitive dog shows.

16 **best practice**
/ (best prak'tis)/

adjective
- Of business practices and procedures, known to produce near-optimum results.

Examples:
But Africa also has the opportunity to leapfrog over traditional solutions and transition rapidly to renewable energy using best-practice models for infrastructure delivery and maintenance. —Vijaya Ramachandran, "Zoellick Goes to Africa," *The Huffington Post*, August 12, 2009

Success-oriented small-business owners are more open to learning how others run their businesses. They actively seek best-practice insights regarding management, business innovation and prospecting, as well as finding, motivating and retaining employees. —Meghan Casserly, "Six Signs of Small-Business Success," *Forbes*, June 30, 2010

The term *best-practice* has lost some of its impact and come to mean something that simply works rather than something that achieves optimum or near-optimum results.

black-market

/ (blak mär'kit)/

noun

1 Trade that is in violation of restrictions, rationing or price controls.

2 The people who engage in such trade (considered as a group), or that sector of the economy.

adjective

1 Traded on the black market.

2 Contraband, bootleg or smuggled.

verb

1 To participate in a black market.

2 To sell in a black market.

Examples:

An investigation into political corruption in New Jersey produced 44 arrests, including a Brooklyn rabbi who was charged with the sale of black-market kidneys. —Dan Collins, "10 Worst Moments in New York Politics," *The Huffington Post*, December 31, 2009

The arrest has reverberated through the Latin American country because the firm, Rosemont Finance Corp., serves as a key U.S. clearing house for dozens of black-market brokerages—trading houses that exploit loopholes to sell dollars despite an official Venezuelan ban on private firms buying and selling currency at unofficial rates. —John Lyons and Jose de Cordoba, "U.S. Seizure Slams Market for Dollars in Venezuela," *The Wall Street Journal*, March 28, 2009

The North Koreans started to obtain Chinese-Pakistani enrichment technology in the early 1990s from the black-market ring headed by Dr. Abdul Qadeer Khan. —Gordon G. Chang, "Nuclear Leak in North Korea," *Forbes*, June 23, 2010

Black in the sense of *black-market* means "illegitimate, illegal, or disgraced."

18 **boilerplate**
/ (boi'lər-plāt͵)/

noun

1 A sheet of steel used in the construction of a boiler.
2 Standard text or program code used routinely and added with a text editor or word processor; text of a legal or official nature added to documents or labels.

adjective

* Describing text of a standard or routine nature.

Examples:

That was boilerplate, of course, but sometimes boilerplate is there for a reason. —Herb Greenberg, "NovaStar Offered Early Clues to Looming Mortgage Tumult," *The Wall Street Journal*, November 24, 2007

And given recent insights into polling data and cell phone users, it's entirely possible that the only thing between a decisive Obama lead coming into October and more election-as-nail-biter boilerplate is the vast left wing wireless network. —John Wihbey, "The Cell Phone Polling Gap: An Artificially 'Close' Race?" *The Huffington Post*, October 1, 2008

A boilerplate is a section of HTML code that is common to many different documents. —"Duplicate Content & Multiple Site Issues," *Search Engine Roundtable*, April 11, 2007

Boilerplate, as meaning "standard text," first referred to filler stories provided on metal plates, used to supply extra copy for newspapers and magazines.

19 bootstrap

/ (boot'strap,) /

noun

1 A loop (leather or other material) sewn at the side or top rear of a boot to help in pulling the boot on.

2 A means of advancing oneself or accomplishing something with little or no aid.

verb
- To help (oneself) with little or no aid from others.

Examples:
These are mostly entrepreneurs and former entrepreneurs who invest in bootstrap companies too young and raw to attract attention and money from professional venture capitalists. —Chris Farrell, "The U.S. Economy Needs a Host of Angel Investors," *Newsweek*, April 19, 2010

During Mr. Schmall's testimony, the Libby defense team is trying to slip that memory defense and the national security information which has already been ruled, in part, to be very limitedly admissible, if at all, into the minds of the jury through a back door and a completely unrelated witness. In effect, as prosecutor Patrick Fitzgerald argued this morning, to "bootstrap" the evidence and the arguments into the case. —Christy Hardin Smith, "Libby Trial: Peeling Back the Layers," *The Huffington Post*, February 11, 2007

In computer programming, *bootstrap* is usually shortened to *boot*, and refers to loading the operating system into the memory of a computer.

20 **bottom-line**
/ (bot'əm līn)/

noun

1 The final balance; the amount of money or profit left after everything has been tallied.

2 The summary or result; the most important information; the upshot; the net-net.

Examples:

The bottom-line is that many blogs have become must-reads on a daily basis for people who closely follow the news and currents, replacing traditional print. —Phillip M. Fogel, "How Social Media Are Changing Money Management," *Forbes*, May 4, 2010

They know that short-sighted competitors will be doing quite the opposite—cutting marketing budgets, depleting their work forces and cutting corners—in a vain attempt to rescue the bottom-line. —Brian Humphries, "Why Corporate Jets Should Still Fly," *The Wall Street Journal*, January 14, 2009

Find your ROI: When preparing to look for a job in a new industry, clarify and focus on the measurable contributions to the bottom-line result you've achieved for your former or current employers, and show how it can work anywhere. — Meredith Haberfeld, "Career Change: 10 Big Steps to a Successful Career Transition," *The Huffington Post*, May 6, 2009

As guardians of power, today's dominant media system is in crisis because it's bottom-line driven, unresponsive to public needs, and concerned only about the interests of wealth and power. —Stephen Lendman, "Reviewing Project Censored's Latest Top 25 Censored Stories," *OpEdNews.com*, October 2, 2009

Bottom-line originated as the literal bottom line of a written income statement or other accounting record.

21 **brainstorming**
/ (brān'stôr,ming)/

noun
- A method of problem solving in which members of a group contribute ideas spontaneously.

Examples:
The whole point of brainstorming is to let creativity shine. —Josh Linkner, "The 10 Commandments of Brainstorming," *Forbes*, April 20, 2010

Others save money by coming up with their own monikers in brainstorming sessions with colleagues and family, or office-wide naming parties. —Suzanne Barlyn, "Name That Firm," *The Wall Street Journal*, March 17, 2008

The next step of brainstorming is to take the free associa-
tion/stream of consciousness list and circle the words that
pertain to the problem, and connect them with "web" lines
into "clusters." —Fredric Lozo, *Sequential Problem Solving*, 1998

The Beatrice Public Schools Board of Education met Tues-
day night for a retreat session to begin brainstorming solutions to problems the district will face in the future. —Chris
Dunker, "School board studies pending problems," *Beatrice Daily Sun*,
February 3, 2010

A *brainstorm* is "a sudden thought or insight, particularly regarding
a long-standing problem." *Brainstorming* is a technique often used
in creative problem solving.

22 brand
/ (brand)/

noun

1 A name, symbol, logo, or other item used to distinguish a
   product or manufacturer from its competitors.
2 A specific product or manufacturer so distinguished.
3 Any specific type or variety of something; a distinct style,
   manner.
4 A product's attributes—name, appearance, reputation,
   and so on—taken collectively and abstractly.

verb
- To associate a product or service with a trademark or other name and related images.

Examples:
An interesting book written by Dr. Nikolaus Eberl and Herman Schoonbee, "Internal Branding: The IziCwe Code," says that "a brand is an expectation of an emotional experience, created by a certain brand promise." —"The New South Africa –A Season of Hope!" ANC *Today*, January 19, 2006

When [Martha] Stewart went to prison as a result of a tussle with Wall Street, there were some who felt the brand would never be able to rebound. To the contrary, the company took on a comeback campaign, identifying new and distinctly on-brand ways to tell its story to appeal to the current and growing house-proud audience. —Allen Adamson, "For Playboy, Chevrolet Corvette: Lessons From Martha Stewart," *Forbes*, July 20, 2010

Brand comes from the Middle English word for *torch*.

23

break-even point

/ (brāk ē'vən point)/

noun

- The point where total costs equal total sales revenue and the company neither makes a profit nor suffers a loss. Sometimes called the *break-even price* or abbreviated as *BEP*.

Examples:

We lowered the cash flow and profitability break-even point of the business by restructuring our approach to member marketing and reducing operating expenses which allowed us to have a profitable fourth quarter despite a significant shift in consumer spending on dining. —"Rewards Network, Inc. Q4 2008 Earnings Call Transcript," *Seeking Alpha*, March 2, 2009

The break-even price (BEP, anything they sell for less than this price, they lose money) of oil, as indicated by the International Monetary Fund (IMF), for Iraq is $94/bbl (or $111), Iran $90/bbl and Venezuela $58/bbl. —Patrick Takahashi, "Will Oil Prices Remain Low for Two Years?" *The Huffington Post*, February 12, 2009

School officials expect to get an increase of $295,000 in BEP funding, an inflationary adjustment for retirement rate increases and health insurance premiums but a smaller in-

crease than the education system might normally expect.
—John Huotari, "School budget talks could be 'eye-opening,'" *Oak Ridger*,
February 18, 2010

Sometimes the *break-even point* is simply referred to as the *break-even*.

bull market
24 / (bool här'kit)/

noun
- A stock market where a majority of investors are buying
  ("bulls"), causing overall stock prices to rise.

Examples:
Oil's collapse this year ended a bull market that began in
2002, when crude traded at $17.85 a barrel. —Mark Williams,
"Crude ends extraordinary volatile year below $45," *South Coast Today*,
January 1, 2009

During the bull market, Deal Toys became so popular they
spawned a cottage industry and stoked duels among banks
vying for creative ideas to memorialize mergers, initial public offerings and other transactions. —Ianthe Jeanne Dugan, "Another Wall Street Casualty: The Art of the 'Deal Toy,'" *The Wall Street
Journal*, February 11, 2009

The opposite of a *bull market* is a *bear market*, in which the majority of investors are selling, causing prices to drop.

25 bureaucracy

/ (byoo-rok′rə-sē)/

noun

1 Government by bureaus; specifically, excessive multiplication of, and concentration of power in, administrative bureaus. The principle of bureaucracy tends to cause official interference in many of the properly private affairs of life, and to the inefficient and obstructive performance of duty through minute subdivision of functions, inflexible formality, and pride of place.

2 The body of officials administering such bureaus, considered collectively.

Examples:

His answer to this quandary has been to use his foreign ministry where a genetically left-leaning foreign service bureaucracy is headed by the notoriously anti-American, anticapitalist intellectual Celso Amorim to burnish his leftist credentials. —Mary Anastasia O'Grady, "Lula's Dance With the Despots," *The Wall Street Journal*, June 14, 2010

Lansley said that he would be cutting out [a billion British pounds] of savings in "bureaucracy" and that in the last

seven years the costs of red tape in the NHS had doubled.
—Randeep Ramesh, "Food Standards Agency to be abolished by health
secretary," *The Guardian*, July 12, 2010

The revolt of the bureaucracy is already underway. —Howard
Fineman, "Bursting Obama's Balloons," *Newsweek*, January 2, 2009

In a *bureaucracy*, one may encounter *red tape*, "a derisive term for
regulations or bureaucratic procedures that are considered excessive or excessively time- and effort-consuming."

26 **business-to-business**
/ (biz'nis too biz'nis)/

adjective
- Of businesses selling to other businesses.

Examples:
A deal would have reduced the Swiss company's annual
revenue by about 20%, but analysts welcomed the merger
plan because margins in the business-to-business chocolate
market are attractive. —Goran Mijuk, "Barry Callebaut, Natra Drop
Chocolate Deal," *The Wall Street Journal*, September 9, 2009

But superstar syndrome, along with sports like auto racing,
golf and tennis that emphasize individual performance and
appeal to a growing middle class that skews toward globalist

business-to-business values, could help cause Brazil to take a back seat to Italy as the world's dominant football [soccer] nation. —Eric Ehrmann, "Brazil: Futebol Before Politics," *The Huffington Post*, May 21, 2010

When they're applied to business-to-business purchases of, say, legal advice, they may lead to double-taxing for one. —Stephane Fitch, "States Eye Service Sales Taxes to Battle Shortfalls," *Forbes*, May 26, 2010

Suppliers, notice how sellers in the business-to-business transaction set themselves up as subordinate to buyers with the idiom supplier, pride themselves on being the single source or the preferred source to the team that is creating this or that service or product at their client/customer. — Chaz Valenza, "Big Greed's Dream," *OpEdNews.com*, July 14, 2009

Business-to-business is often referred to as *B2B*.

(27) **buy·in**

/ (bī in)/

noun

● Support; agreement; approval; blessing (in a secular sense).

Examples:

By engaging the board first in setting the criteria and then in refreshing them each year, you create buy-in and alignment among the jury that will select the next leader. —Stephen A. Miles and Nathan Bennett, "How the SEC Just Changed Succession Planning: Part II," *Forbes*, November 18, 2009

The contest puts a premium, Obama administration officials say, on bold innovation as well as buy-in from teachers' unions and local school boards. —Nick Anderson, "Washington area vies for Round 2 of Race to the Top funds," *The Washington Post*, April 19, 2010

Buy-in differs from *buyout*, which is "the acquisition of a controlling interest in a business or corporation by outright purchase or by purchase of a majority of issued shares of stock."

28 **cannibalize**

/ (kan'ə-bə-līz,)/

verb

- To remove parts of (a machine, etc.) for use in other similar machines, or, by extension, to deprive one area of vital resources, such as personnel, equipment, or funding, for use in another area.

Examples:

And now we arrive at a juncture where the budget crisis ostensibly is being used as cover to "cannibalize" the state's education system, quite possibly in an irreparable manner. —Randall Amster, "Worst in Class: How Education in Arizona Became an Economic Casualty," *The Huffington Post*, February 5, 2009

Fearing that the Internet would "cannibalize" print sales, Condé Nast built sites for most magazines that seemed more like teasers than destinations—they existed online simply so that readers might be enticed to click on the "subscribe" button to get all the good print stuff. —Gillian Reagan, "More Than Fashionably Late, Condé Nast Hits the Internet," *The New York Observer*, October 27, 2009

Barbour says he doesn't like the idea of the state luring citizens to play the lottery and that he believes a lottery would "cannibalize" existing casinos' gross receipts. —Sid Salter, "Lottery bill: State gave away store to casino interests," *The Meridian Star*, February 10, 2010

Cannibalize comes from the Carib word *karibna*, meaning "person." Christopher Columbus thought the Caribs were cannibals, and brought the word back to Europe with him.

29   **capitalization**

/ (kap͟i-tl-i-zā'shən)/

noun

1 The act of capitalizing. The application of wealth as capital, especially in large amounts, to the purposes of trade, manufactures, etc.

2 The act of computing or realizing the present value of a periodical payment.

Examples:

Today Apple has more cash and marketable securities than the market value of Dell. Apple was nearly bankrupt in 2000; now its market capitalization is almost $200 billion—within striking distance of Microsoft, whose market cap has fallen 40%. —Adam Hartung, "A Key to a Successful Business Plan," *Forbes*, December 7, 2009

India's biggest retailer by market capitalization is now aiming to add 2.5 million square feet of retail space—rather than the earlier planned 4 million square feet —in the year beginning July 1. —Rumman Ahmed, "Pantaloon Cuts Store Expansion Target," *The Wall Street Journal*, March 19, 2009

A former Bush-administration official says that the last thing the president wanted was to be at the center of another corporate scandal, and if you were looking for likely candidates, how could you miss Fannie and Freddie, with their longtime critics and thin capitalization? —Bethany McClean, "Fannie Mae's Last Stand," *Vanity Fair*, February 2009

Capitalization comes from *capital*, "money and wealth," which comes from the Latin word *capitālis*, meaning "head, money laid out."

30 code-of-conduct
/ (kōd uv kən-dukt')/

noun
* A set of rules to guide behavior and decisions in a specified situation.

Examples:
A day before she took the helm, she and outgoing CEO Mr. Glasscock had to announce another surprise management shakeup: Mr. Colby, the finance chief, had agreed to resign because of an undisclosed code-of-conduct violation. It later emerged that Mr. Colby was entangled in multiple romantic relationships, including one with a former employee. —Vanessa Fuhrmans, "Angela Braly Tops the List," *The Wall Street Journal*, November 19, 2007

The organization has conducted code-of-conduct monitoring for multinational companies and tripartite forums on labor issues in local industries. —John Tepper Marlin, "Green Edge

8–Saving Lives on Farms in Latin America–Cultivar," *The Huffington Post*, September 1, 2008

A few times over the years, risqué couples have been spotted through the hotel windows. But they don't make you sign anything when they check you in here. There's no code-of-conduct sheet with your room key. Common sense pretty much prevails. —Tyler Kepner, "A Room with a View in Toronto," *The New York Times*, March 8, 2009

Behavior that goes against the *code-of-conduct* of a company may not be against the law, but may be subject to disciplinary action.

31 cold-calling
/ (kōld kô'ling)/

noun, verb

- The practice of making unsolicited telephone calls to potential clients, voters, or other groups to drum up customers or investigate intentions.

Examples:

As odd as it sounds, many salesmen are so afraid of getting shot down that they wait for clients to come to them rather than cold-calling or being aggressive. —Shaun Rein, "How a Dating Fiasco Taught Me to Be a Salesman," *Forbes*, July 12, 2010

After cold-calling several foreign newspaper bureaus to ask if she could help out, a reporter at the *Washington Post* took her on and put her to work gathering quotes and monitoring the Chinese-language press. —Leslie Hook and Joseph Sternberg, "Confessions of Two Unpaid Interns," *The Wall Street Journal*, April 8, 2010

Last month, celebrity trainer Tracy Anderson was reportedly having difficulties getting people to sign up for her new $900-per-month Tribeca gym, where her most prominent client, the actress Gwyneth Paltrow, is also a partner. . . . According to Page Six, the gym's reps were even cold-calling people and asking them to come in for a meeting. —Irina Aleksander, "Still Gym-less, Celebrity Trainer Tracy Anderson Teaches at the Marriott," *The New York Observer*, April 7, 2009

Cold-calling has the sense of calling potential clients out of the blue, without any "warming up."

32   collaborative
/ (kə-lab'ə-rə-tiv)/

adjective
- Of, relating to, or done by collaboration.

noun
- An organized group of people or entities who collaborate toward a particular goal.

38

Examples:

Should external innovators be organized in collaborative communities or competitive markets? —Frank T. Rothaermel and Andrew M. Hess, "Finding an Innovation Strategy That Works," *The Wall Street Journal*, August 17, 2009

It's an approach to work that's about engaging people in collaborative activities. —Mac Slocum, "In Defense of Games at Work," *Forbes*, July 22, 2010

The data, they added, should be utilized in collaborative research between the universities of J&K and the proposed Directorate. —Vivek Suri, "Geo-scientists recommend resuming of oil, hydrocarbons exploration in Kashmir," *Ground Report*, May 21, 2009

This stark reality confounds environmentalists and amplifies their differences with Labor, at times engendering tension within collaborative efforts such as the Blue Green and Apollo Alliances that embrace both constituencies. —Marco Trbovich, "Obama's Global Challenge," *The Huffington Post*, December 11, 2008

In business, working *collaboratively* is opposed to working *competitively*, or striving against one another to reach a certain goal. *Collaborative* comes from the Latin word *collabōrāre*, which contains the root *labor*, "toil."

33

commoditization

/ (kə-mädˌi-tə-zā' sh ən)/

noun

* The transformation of something into a commodity, or undifferentiated goods characterized by a low profit margin, as distinguished from branded products.

Examples:

Usually, commoditization is the result of a failure to act early enough. —Richard D'Aveni, "Are You Facing a Commodity Trap?" *Entrepreneur*, December 1, 2009

The democratization of information may result in commoditization of brands as consumers make purchase decisions by searching for the lowest-priced product. —Avi Dan, "Why Brands Should Embrace Technological Change," *Advertising Age*, January 19, 2010

In an internal memo that later became public, Mr. Schultz conceded earlier this year that there had been a "watering down of the Starbucks experience, and what some might call the commoditization of our brand." —Matthew Rees, "The Fresh-Roasted Smell of Success," *The Wall Street Journal*, November 7, 2007

When I used to hang around Brooklyn hipster bars . . . there was one tattoo type my fellow denizens sported that was meant to be ironic. . . . I'm speaking of the bar code tattoo, a commentary on the commoditization of the self through the universal "UPC" code affixed to product packaging. — Noah Mallin, "Social Media: Soon, Our Facebook Profiles Might Follow Us Offline Too," *The Huffington Post*, March 24, 2010

Commoditization comes from the Latin word *commoditās*, meaning "convenient."

34

conflict of interest
/ (kon'flikt uv in'trist)

noun

- A situation in which someone in a position of trust, such as a lawyer, insurance adjuster, politician, executive or director of a corporation, or medical research scientist or physician, has competing professional or personal interests.

Examples:
Virginia law allows a legislative ethics panel to refer complaints to the attorney general if an inquiry shows that a legislator willfully violated conflict-of-interest law. —Anita Kumar, "Legislators reject McDonnell ethics amendment; governor mulls bill," *The Washington Post*, April 22, 2010

Government rules empower ethics officials to waive conflict-of-interest concerns in cases where, for instance, Hillary [Clinton's] continued participation on a specific issue "outweighs" such fears. —Mark Hosenball, "Sorry, No Fireworks This Time," *Newsweek*, January 10, 2009

The White House needs to go back and look at the conflict-of-interest riddled Fannie Mae debacle, in which public interest and private gain got stewed together and undermined the interests of American citizens. —Steve Clemons, "Communications Corruption at White House," *The Huffington Post*, April 2, 2010

Nowadays the conflict-of-interest cops would come down hard on any editor who dared to permit a Broadway director to double as a drama critic. —Terry Teachout, "Opinion Born of Experience," *The Wall Street Journal*, April 4, 2009

Conflict of interest may apply to all individuals in situations where there is a conflict between one's private interests and public obligations.

35 **contrarian**
/ (kən-trâr'ē-ən)/

noun

1 A financial investor who tends to have an opinion of market trends at variance with most others.

2 A person who expresses a contradicting viewpoint, especially one who denounces the majority persuasion.

Examples:

Atkins acolytes such as Gary Taubes . . . writes that exercise does not help you lose weight—being a contrarian is one thing, being obtuse is another. —Dr. Dean Ornish, "All Calories Are Not the Same!" *The Huffington Post*, March 6, 2009

As one wag pointed out, "When someone cries 'fire' in a crowded theater, a contrarian is the person who first checks to see if there really is a fire before rushing to the exit." — Richard Wise, "Only a Maverick," *OpEdNews.com*, October 31, 2008

Being a true contrarian is very difficult, not just because it demands that one correctly identify the prevailing trends and find points of extreme but also because it requires that one have the mental and emotional fortitude to go against the crowd and "stand alone." —"Sentiment Overview: Starting the Year in a Bullish Mood," *Seeking Alpha*, January 3, 2010

Contrarian comes from *contrary*, "given to contradiction; acting in opposition," which comes from the Latin word *contrārius*, meaning "against."

36 **cost-effective**

/ (kôst i-fek'tiv)/

adjective

* Returning a benefit that justifies the initial investment; economical.

Examples:

Some marketers are taking steps they hope will make their advertising more cost-effective, such as using in-store displays and Internet marketing instead of TV ads, said Shaun Rein, founder of Shanghai-based consulting firm China Market Research. —Carlos Tejada and Sky Canaves, "Lunar New Year May Be a Tough Holiday for Sales," *The Wall Street Journal*, January 21, 2009

Nurses do provide quality care. They help reduce costs through increased preventive care, and they deliver cost-effective primary care, along with physicians, especially in the underserved areas. —"Roadblocks to Health Reform; Dow Hits 12-Year Low; President Obama Hosts White House Summit on Health Care Reform," CNN Transcripts, March 5, 2009

Creating an Open 311 system is quite simply the most cost-effective way for the city to improve on its existing 311 system, because it transfers the costs of these improvements to third party entities seeking to build on top of the 311 platform. —Micah L. Sifry, "An Open 311 System for the City of New York—A Letter to Mayor Bloomberg," *Tech President*, May 28, 2009

The opposite of *cost-effective* is *cost-prohibitive*.

37   **decentralization**
/ (dē-senˌtrəl-i-zā'sh ən)/

noun
* The act of decentralizing, or the state of being decentralized; specifically, the act or principle of removing local or special functions of the corporation from the immediate direction or control of the central office. Often used in a political sense.

Examples:
The solution lies in decentralization, putting decisions into the hands of smaller communities of peoples, then building communities of communities. —Jim Miles, "Book Review–American Empire and the Commonwealth of God," *OpEdNews.com*, October 5, 2007

The decentralization is the work of a compact minority of leaders who, when forced to subordinate themselves in the central executive of the party as a whole, prefer to withdraw to their own local spheres of action (minor state, province, or commune). —Robert Michels, *Political Parties; a Sociological Study of the Oligarchical Tendencies of Modern Democracy,* 1916

For the Kurds, the preferred alternative to decentralization is not greater unity but separation. —Peter W. Galbraith, "Biden's Iraq Plan May Have Helped," *The Wall Street Journal,* September 12, 2008

After all, decentralization is the highest form of democratization.—"Dealing with a New Russia," *Newsweek,* September 2, 1991

Decentralization is the opposite of *centralization,* "the act of transferring local administration to the central seat of power."

(38)

/ (di-sizh'ən trē)/

noun
- A visualization of a complex decision-making situation in which the possible decisions and their likely outcomes are organized in the form of a graph that resembles a tree.

Examples:
Here is a basic decision-tree analysis that will allow you to deconstruct the problem into components, weigh the relative significance of the parts, assign possibilities to them and reach a conclusion. —Robert Bovarnick, "When Is Litigation Worth the Hassle?" *Forbes,* July 21, 2010

The thought of inviting another woman's children into my world–just as choices and outcomes began to make sense–might not have seemed rational. I did not make the decision lightly. Although the faulty logic of my opening syllogism appealed to the romantic in me, it was certainly not how I constructed my decision-tree. —Evelyn Sharenov, "Confessions of a Stepmom," *Tehran Times*, August 4, 2010

In addition to the *decision tree*, another decision-making process is *backward induction*, "the process of reasoning backward in time, from the end of a problem or situation, to determine a sequence of optimal actions."

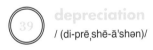

39 depreciation

/ (di-prē͵shē-ā'shən)/

noun
1 The act of lessening or bringing down price or value.
2 A fall in value; reduction of worth.

Examples:
Finally, leasing encourages people to get a new car every few years, during a period when vehicle loss in value, known as depreciation, is greatest. —Anthony Giorgianni, "Lost your job? Good luck getting out of that car lease," *Consumer Reports*, July 1, 2010

Now the dismal arithmetic of euro depreciation is quite simple—expected further depreciation will keep investible funds out of Europe and threatens to unleash a vicious cycle of declining competitiveness and low investment that will erode living standards—not just for the fiscally profligate, but for all eurozone nations. —Jagadeesh Gokhale, "The E.U.'s Aggressive Bailout Plan," *Forbes*, May 11, 2010

While the "pace of depreciation has slowed visibly in recent months on signs of stabilizing economies and markets," the report finds, "additional depreciation is still possible in the near term if global demand wanes further." —Michael S. Arnold, "Asian Stocks Show Signs of Recovery, ADB Report Says," *The Wall Street Journal*, April 20, 2009

The opposite of *depreciation* is *appreciation*, "a rising in value; increase of value."

40 depression
/ (di-presh'ən)/

noun

1 A period of major economic contraction.
2 Four consecutive quarters of negative, real GDP growth.

Examples:

While not having another depression is a good thing, all indications are that unless the government does much more than is currently planned to help the economy recover, the job market—a market in which there are currently six times as many people seeking work as there are jobs on offer—will remain terrible for years to come. —Paul Krugman, "Mission Not Accomplished," *OpEdNews.com*, October 2, 2009

But surely the political will to punish the banks that led the country to the brink of a depression is at least as strong as the will to reform health care. —Eric Schurenberg, "Four Questions About Obama's Financial Reforms," *The Huffington Post*, September 14, 2009

The most common definition of a depression is a long period in which GDP or consumption declines at least 10%. —Michael J. Boskin, "Obama's Economic Fish Stories," *The Wall Street Journal*, July 21, 2010

The Great *Depression* was a major economic collapse that lasted from 1929 to 1941 in the United States and many other countries.

41

disconnect

/ (dis̩kə-nekt')/

noun

• A lack of connection or accord; a mismatch.

Examples:

Bill Maher laid into the tea party movement and the American people for what he described as their disconnect from the reality of the nation's finances. —"Bill Maher Blasts Tea Baggers for Ignoring Defense Spending," *The Huffington Post*, April 24, 2010

Adding to the disconnect is the fact that the railroads deem a train late only if it reaches its terminus more than 5 minutes 59 seconds after the scheduled arrival time. —Michael M. Grynbaum and Robert Gebeloff, "95% of Trains Are on Time? Riders Beg to Differ," *The New York Times*, July 26, 2010

Disconnect, as a noun meaning "discord" or "lack of understanding," may have originated from the sense of a break in a telephone connection, therefore a break in communication.

42

disintermediate
/ (dis-in‚tər-mē‚dē-āt)/

verb

- To carry out disintermediation, the removal of funds from a financial institution such as a bank for direct purchase of financial instruments, or the removal of an intermediary from a commercial transaction.

Examples:

TV sets that connect directly to the web will eventually disintermediate local TV and radio stations and cable systems, just like craigslist. com and the web has ruined the dead-tree newspaper business. —Charles Warner, "FCC Reviews Buggy Whip Rules," *The Huffington Post*, May 27, 2010

Or to put it another way: the functionality of Web 2.0 can disintermediate content, but it seems apparent that the navigational skills of publishers and librarians are still needed in the vast sea stretching before us. —"Navigating the vast wasteland of YouTube," *The Chicago Blog*, 2008

Hosts David Asman and Liz Claman practically crowned the mayor an economic genius after he told them he's asking for wage concessions from labor groups, combining departments and trying to "disintermediate" bureaucracies. —

Heather Knight, "Economic crisis? What economic crisis?" *San Francisco Chronicle*, March 4, 2009

One of the misconceptions of the Software-as-a-Service (SaaS) and broader cloud computing market is that these new Web-based services will "disintermediate" the channel because of their simpler, more user-friendly solutions, and direct sales and delivery business models. —Jeffrey M. Kaplan, "SaaS and Cloud Computing: The Channel Is Far From Dead," *E-Commerce Times*, April 10, 2009

Disintermediate contains the Latin word *medius,* meaning "middle."

43 diversification
/ (dī-vər-si-fi-kā'shən)/

noun

1 The act of changing forms or qualities, or of making various: as, *diversification* of labor.
2 Diversity or variation; change; alteration: as, "*diversification* of voice."

Examples:
There were grocers and merchants, with every variety of goods and wares for sale; there were banks and bankers; there was all the diversification of industry that a thriving, industrious, and intelligent community required; not estab-

lished by protection nor by government aid, but growing naturally out of the wants and necessities of the people. —Frank H. Hurd, "A Tariff for Revenue Only," *American Eloquence: Studies in American Political History*, 1896

Along with diversification of assets—stocks, bonds, cash—maintain diversification in the stock market, as well. —Dave Kansas, "What Do I Do Now?" *The Wall Street Journal*, April 7, 2009

The problem with diversification is that it works wonderfully in smoothing out volatility, until it doesn't. —Gregg S. Fisher, "How to Profit from Investment 'Losers,'" *Forbes*, March 30, 2010

The city's fortunes are still linked to Gulf oil and its selling price, and so its vaunted diversification is of limited use. —Jennifer Nix, "Unconventional Wisdom on Dubai," *The Huffington Post*, September 16, 2009

Diversification is also "a corporate strategy in which a company acquires or establishes a business other than that of its current product."

44

downsize

/ (doun'sīz,)/

verb

1 To reduce in size or number.
2 To reduce the workforce of.

3 To terminate the employment of.

Examples:

The evening before school began, Ms. Walters drove 45 minutes to an RV campground to deliver a scientific calculator and other essential school supplies to Cody Curry, 14, who lives with his mother, Dawn, and his brother, Zack, 11, in a camper. Mrs. Curry had to downsize from a trailer, she said, when her work as a sales clerk was cut to two days a week. —Arianna Huffington, "The Story That Made Me Tear Up My Prepared Speech at a Big Education Conference," *The Huffington Post*, September 9, 2009

Salyer said he saw customers who told him they'd have never considered buying a new car. But they couldn't pass up a deal—and an opportunity to downsize from a gas-guzzler with the memory of $4 per gallon gas still fresh. —Ron Maloney, "Area dealers weigh in on stimulus program," *Seguin Gazette-Enterprise*, August 26, 2009

That Ted, the union guy at the plant Lucy plans to downsize, is perhaps not a perfect match never even occurs to Blanche, who like all Minnesotans and most Dakotans is just plain nice. —Roger Ebert, "New in Town," *Chicago Sun-Times*, January 28, 2009

Downsizing has now been replaced by another euphemism, *rightsizing*.

45 downstream

/ (doun strēm)/

adverb

- With or in the direction of the current of a stream, or, of a process, happening closer to the point of sale rather than the point of production.

Examples:

According to FairPensions, about 11m litres of contaminated water leaks into surrounding rivers and groundwater each day, containing arsenic, mercury and various carcinogens that have been linked to elevated rates of cancer in downstream communities. —Richard Wachman, "Anger grows across the world at the real price of 'frontier oil'," *The Guardian*, June 20, 2010

Just as the totals for "Gross Domestic Product" can go up to reflect the increased spending caused by a devastating hurricane, the economic activity generated by the oil and gas industry could include the hospital visits by asthma sufferers–by the people in downstream First Nations communities whose cancer rates have skyrocketed since tar sands development began. —James Hoggan, "Oil Sands Newest PR Push Doomed to Fail–Again," *The Huffington Post*, April 20, 2010

The goal is to block the chain reaction of events leading to uncontrolled cell growth somewhere downstream from the one (or more) genes that are causing the problem. —David Brown, "War against cancer has more than one target," *The Washington Post*, April 27, 2010

Some of that is due to the profits squeeze in "downstream" gasoline retailing. —Brett Arends, "In Defense of Oil Stocks," *The Wall Street Journal*, June 25, 2008

The opposite of *downstream* is *upstream*.

46 | **due diligence**
/ (do͞o dil'ə-jəns)/

noun

• A legally binding process during which a potential buyer evaluates the assets and liabilities of a company.

Examples:

The Quebec government said that, following a due-diligence review, it has determined that the $3.2 billion Canadian-dollar (US $3.15 billion) deal would have required more investment by provincially owned Hydro-Quebec than previously thought and would have involved more risk. —Edward Welsch, "Hydro-Quebec Cancels $3 Billion Deal," *The Wall Street Journal*, March 25, 2010

The leading Tory blogger Tim Montgomerie said: "Big questions need to be asked about [Tory HQ] failing to carry out due diligence on this appointment." —Allegra Stratton and Haroon Siddique, "David Rowland: red faces at Tory HQ as next treasurer quits," *The Guardian*, August 19, 2010

Travel/aviation needs the same business processes that you use for your other business decisions. Giving it due diligence and applying evaluative and ongoing analytical processes, helps assure that your ongoing needs are met and that your spends and benefits are optimized. —Jeffrey Reich, "How Do You Ensure the Optimal Air Travel Solution for Your Company?" *Forbes*, August 19, 2010

As for non-"Twilight" fans, "Vampires Suck" does its due diligence by tossing in a few more general pop culture gags, riffing predictably on everyone from the Kardashians to Chris Brown. —Jen Chaney, "'Twilight' parody 'Vampires Suck' lives up to its name," *The Washington Post*, August 19, 2010

Due diligence also has a general meaning of researching and analyzing a situation before coming to a decision.

47 earned media
/ (ûrn'd mē'dē-ə)/

noun
- Publicity for political campaigns gained through newspaper articles, TV news stories, Web news, letters to the editor, op-ed pieces, and "fast polls" on TV and the Web.

Examples:

A few months ago, McCain's campaign manager was quoted in the *New York Times* calling him "the best earned-media candidate in history." For those unfamiliar with the lingo, "earned media" means press coverage. —Paul Waldman, "McCain Thinks the Media Is Out to Get Him . . . Try Not to Laugh," *The Huffington Post*, August 20, 2008

Because earned-media postings come from real people, not marketers, consumers trust them more and view them as a major influence on purchase decisions. —"Making the Most of Earned Media," *eMarketer*, February 11, 2010

Because success in social media is more "earned media" than "paid media" —and isn't earned media what great PR companies deliver? It is obvious to nearly every advertiser that to be effective they need to be in people's social content, rather than simply being placed next to people's social content. —Joe Marchese, "The Future Agency of Record Will Be Social," *Online Spin*, February 3, 2009

Earned media is essentially "free" media, as opposed to advertising, which is normally paid for.

48 end-to-end

/ (end-too-end)/

adjective

1 Arranged such that each end of a given item is adjacent to one end of a different item.

2 From one end to the other.

Examples:
Chief Executive Michael Klayko said the company had record revenue during the period, driven by strong demand for its end-to-end networking products. —Kerry E. Grace, "Brocade Swings to Loss on Write-Downs," *The Wall Street Journal*, May 21, 2009

To create such a lean and secure service required an end-to-end solution, with both the device, the BlackBerry, and the server hosting the user's e-mail being able to understand each other. —Richard Wray, "How BlackBerry developed its mobile phone and networks," *The Guardian*, August 2, 2010

The project would address ways "to guarantee the freedom to connect, the need for open, end-to-end networks, and the free flow of data and communications across borders on a unified Internet." —Monroe Price, "The Battle Over Internet Regulatory Paradigms," *The Huffington Post*, August 3, 2010

It's the cumulative, "end-to-end" impact of these separate steps that apparently create a self-reinforcing virtuous circle for enterprise mobility performance, according to the Borg. —John Cox, "How to best manage enterprise mobility," *Network World*, July 7, 2010

End-to-end is a type of systems design in both technology and manufacturing.

49 entrepreneur
/ (on̩trə-prə-nûr' *or* on̩trə-prə-noor')/

noun

1 A person who organizes and operates a business venture and assumes much of the associated risk.

2 A person who organizes a risky activity of any kind and acts substantially in the manner of a business entrepreneur.

Examples:

Venture capitalists, angel investors and banks sometimes swoop in to help out a business at the start, but more often than not an entrepreneur is on his or her own unless they can catch investors' attention. —Andrew Beattie, "Four Big Businesses Built with Small Cash," *Forbes*, June 7, 2010

If the entrepreneur is the archetypal figure of the age of security who still respected "the boundary between property and speculation," the new archetype of the age of securitisation—the arbitrageur—no longer does so. —"Capitalism, Biotechnology, Securitisation and Other Scary Words!" *Mute Magazine*, October 21, 2008

John V. Walsh marvels at Sarkozy's insistence that the entrepreneur is the source of wealth until he gets around to proposing a lengthening of the work week again when suddenly he discovers that it is labor that produces wealth. — John V. Walsh, "Bossnapping," *Counterpunch*, April 13, 2009

Entrepreneur is from the French word *entreprendre*, "to undertake," and is related to *enterprise*, "an undertaking or project, especially a daring and courageous one."

50   **face time**
(fās tīm)/

noun

● Time spent talking face-to-face with another person or group of people, as opposed to e-mail or other forms of communication. Also *face-time*.

Examples:

Finally, at last week's nuclear summit, 47 world leaders scrambled to get as much face-time with the U.S. president as they could and, in between such efforts, discuss ways to keep bomb-grade nuclear material out of the hands of the wrong people (al-Qaeda, the tea party movement). —John Feffer, "Nuclear Follies," *The Huffington Post*, April 20, 2010

Assess opportunities realistically and do not feign interest in a job that you don't intend to follow through on simply to get face-time with a recruiter. —Caroline Nahas, "Reaching Out to Recruiters in a Down Economy," *The Wall Street Journal*, April 16, 2009

Face time is somewhat analogous to *quality time*, "time spent by working parents with their children, especially time given over to productive or creative attention."

51 **feature creep**

/ (fē'chər krēp)/

noun

- The tendency of a design project or product cycle to accumulate more and more features or details, rather than to be completed and released at a more basic level.

Examples:

Many new companies looking to compete in a given space choose to first copy basic competitor features to level the playing field. Only at this point do they integrate their own functionality and incorporate what they think the consumer will want. This tactic isn't rare by any means, but it may bring about feature creep and maybe even an inferior overall offering. —Aidan Henry, *MappingTheWeb*, August 12, 2008

I think feature creep is very seductive. When we go into a camera store, we all gravitate towards the most complex camera, which has the most dials and selections on it, because that must be the best camera. —Vivek Kaul, "HR needs to simplify the complexities that have crept into it: Marc Effron," *Daily News & Analysis*, August 16, 2010

Ironically however, Google has been delivering a constant stream of chaotic feature creep and announced that "everything" is coming to Google Apps. At what point will

Google have too many features or in fact the right ones? —
Nick Eaton, "Frustrated Microsoft calls Google Apps today's 'New Coke,'"
Seattle PI Blogs, August 4, 2010

A synonym for *feature creep* is *creeping elegance*.

52 **fiscal year**

/ (fis'kəl yîr)/

noun

- An accounting period of one year, not necessarily coin-
  ciding with the calendar year. Often abbreviated *FY*.

Examples:

After all, the President's budget package enacted last fall
made a much publicized "down payment" on eliminating
the deficit; and Clinton's insistence in his fiscal year 1995
budget proposal on maintaining the cuts he earlier promised
suggests a clear departure from the complacency of the last
twelve years. —Peter G. Peterson, "Entitlement Reform: The Way to
Eliminate the Deficit," *The New York Review of Books*, April 7, 1994

Cardinal Health rose 77 cents, or 2.1%, to 36.71 after the
drug wholesaler cut its fiscal-year earnings outlook because
of hospital customers "spending constraints." —Rob Curran,
"Sears and Shaw Rally, but Wal-Mart Weighs," *The Wall Street Journal*,
January 9, 2009

Virginia's spending on bottled water totaled at least $158,000 in FY 2009, and another $126,000 last year, reports the *Post*'s Anita Kumar. —Paige Winfield Cunningham, "Virginia state workers: Bottled up no more," *The Washington Post*, July 15, 2010

Fiscal years differ depending on country and business sector. For the United States, the *fiscal year* generally starts October 1 and ends September 30 of the following year.

53

flow chart
/ (flō chärt)/

noun
- A schematic representation of how the different stages in a process are interconnected.

Examples:
But we're just getting this mysterious, time-traveling party started. Next: a flow chart (guaranteed not to make your brain hurt) explaining how all the castaways are connected, which is followed by an oral history of how it all began— the making of the pilot episode of *Lost*. —"This week's cover: The end of 'Lost,'" *Entertainment Weekly*, May 6, 2010

The flow chart lays out a range of possible responses to a blog post. Airmen can offer a "factual and well-cited response [that] is not factually erroneous, a rant or rage, bashing or negative in nature." They can "let the post stand—no response." Or they can "fix the facts," offering up fresh perspective. —Noah Shachtman, "Air Force Releases 'Counter-Blog' Marching Orders," *Wired*, January 6, 2009

This means that the various public bathrooms in the lab areas feature signs to help reduce user error. One, in the bathroom reserved for women, has a useful flow chart explaining steps that one could take: Flush before, to make sure it's working; flush at an intermediate point; flush after. —Peggy Delaney, "A word about toilets on a research ship," *Scientific American*, April 3, 2009

In addition to a *flow chart*, other types of schematic representations include a *bar chart*, *line chart*, *pie chart*, a *histogram*—an upright bar chart—and a *cartogram*, a maplike graph.

framework
/ (frām wûrk)/

noun

1 A structure or fabric for inclosing or supporting anything; a frame; a skeleton: as, the *framework* of a building; the bones are the *framework* of the body.
2 Structure; constitution; adjusted arrangement; system.

Examples:

The Kyoto protocol has the advantage of being established and understood—but it may not be the only framework that will ensure a fair and efficient outcome. —"Climate experts' forum: the Kyoto question," *Financial Times*, December 15, 2009

The Cynefin framework is frequently (and legitimately) used as a categorisation model around the four domains of simple, complicated, complex and chaotic. —Dave Snowden, "Origins of Cynefin," *Cognitive Edge*, July 11, 2010

So what you need is a mental or process framework that allows your group to kill off ideas and get to the right strategy for that time and that situation. —Nilofer Merchant, "Kill Your Darlings," *Forbes.com*, October 7, 2009

Framework is made up of *frame* plus *work*. *Frame* comes from the Middle English word *framen*, "to further," while *work* comes from the Old English *weorc*, "work."

Gantt chart

/ (gant chärt)/

noun

- A graphical representation of the tasks and resources needed to complete a job or project, which may show ranges of possible start and end dates and the relationships between tasks; used to pinpoint bottlenecks and assign priorities.

Examples:

When I'm planning, I am trying to answer questions like: How many days are available, including weekends? When are critical deliverables? . . . One way to do this is to use a long timeline, like a Gantt chart. All the days line up one after the other in a long horizontal format, which makes it easy to see how long something takes; distance is directly equatable to duration. This is great in theory, but the Gantt chart lacks compactness and is cumbersome to use because you can't *see everything* at once. —David Seah, "Compact Calendar 2010," *David Seah: Better Living Through New Media*, December 11, 2009

Jon is a flight control engineer and produced a Gantt chart to schedule all preparation work. It is unclear how well it was adhered to. —Justin Goh, "Building the dream," *Windy Citizen*, September 3, 2008

The *Gantt chart* was developed by Henry Laurence *Gantt*, an early twentieth-century American engineer.

56 glass ceiling
/ (glas sē'ling)/

noun

* An unwritten, uncodified barrier to further promotion or progression for a member of a specific demographic group.

Examples:

But I thought [Hillary Clinton] looked, still, just a little bit shocked as she reminded her erstwhile supporters, in terms that wobbled with a palpable electric charge between ultimate vanity and ultimate self-negation, that the primary season had not been about her, but about issues of importance to all women, to everyone. There had been, we were reminded once again, eighteen million cracks put into the glass ceiling by her candidacy. —Michael Chabon, "Obama & the Conquest of Denver," *The New York Review of Books*, October 9, 2008

Even women who eschew children, or regretfully end up without them, face glass ceiling bias once they pass age thirty and gain the credentials to join the big leagues. The first I call Prove It Again!, which reflects bias that stems from the fact that women, in high-status historically male jobs, often have to give far more evidence of competence than do similarly situated men. —Joan Williams, "The New Normal: Die Childless at Thirty," *The Huffington Post*, October 21, 2009

The term *glass ceiling* seems to have originated in the United States in the mid-1980s.

57 globalize
/ (glō'bə-līz,) /

verb
* To make something global in scope.

Examples:
[S]pecializing in high tech products would also seem logical, but Japan's global market share "has rapidly declined" and low levels of profitability suggest that the business model for Japanese industries has "caused them to lag behind the world." In response to these challenges, government officials told me last week that the broad strategy is to globalize Japan, making its social systems, ports, and infrastructure attractive to businesses that create value and jobs. —Devin Stewart, "Will a Rudderless Japan Drift into Crisis?" *The Huffington Post*, July 15, 2010

Since then, the firm has sought to globalize its culture, integrating Lehman bankers and naming former Lehman Brothers executive Jasjit "Jesse" Bhattal as chief operation officer of the firm's new global wholesale division. —Ellen Sheng, "Nomura May Join KEB Bid," *The Wall Street Journal*, June 16, 2010

New administrative support features . . . include . . . the ability to "globalize"–make available to all document types–metadata fields that are selection lists. —"EZContentManager Gets New Features," *Information Technology News*, January 26, 2010

Globalize is the verb form of the adjective *global*, meaning "concerning all parts of the world; relating to an entire document, file, or program."

58   **golden parachute**
/ (gōl'dən par'ə-shōōt͵)/

noun

- An agreement between a company and an employee, usually an executive, specifying that the employee will receive certain significant benefits if employment is terminated.

Examples:

Despite their clear leadership failure, AIG executives still feel entitled to outlandish compensation and golden-parachute severance payments. —Eric C. Anderson, "AIG and the Season of Greed," *The Huffington Post*, December 7, 2009

That program, which has invested nearly $200 billion in more than 300 financial institutions, imposes some modest pay restrictions, including a ban on so-called golden-parachute severance payments for top executives. —Deborah Solomon, "Treasury to Outline Bank Plan Next Week," *The Wall Street Journal*, February 3, 2009

In addition to *golden parachutes*, companies may offer a *golden hello*, "a payment offered to an employee as an inducement to join, especially if currently working for a competitor," a *golden handshake*, "a generous severance payment, especially as an inducement to leave employment," or *golden handcuffs*, "any arrangement or agreement designed to provide extremely favorable benefits or pay, so as to discourage participant from wanting to leave, especially to retain a choice employee."

59

hedge fund
/ (hej fund)/

noun
- Any unregistered investment fund, often characterized by unconventional strategies (i.e., strategies other than investing long only in bonds, equities, or money markets).

Examples:
They do seem determined to be activist trustees, able and willing to back their preferences with immense sums (they

rounded up an astonishing $5.7 million from assorted stock-brokers and hedge fund operators for the paean to Hamilton), and it would be naive to assume they will not remain influential players. —David Brion Davis and Louise Mirrer, "'That Hamilton Man': An Exchange," *The New York Review of Books*, May 26, 2005

For starters, the limits seem to apply only to "senior executives"—the chief executive, chief financial officer and the like—and not to many of the people who can earn the really big bucks on Wall Street, like traders, hedge-fund managers and the mad scientists who cooked up all those derivatives that almost destroyed the world financial system. —Jason Zweig, "Pay Collars Won't Hold Back Wall Street's Big Dogs," *The Wall Street Journal*, February 7, 2009

Hedge funds are so named because they are supposed to be hedged–or "offset by another financial asset"–from risk.

60 hyperlocal
/ (hī'pər lō'kəl)/

adjective
- Providing coverage of a very small area, on a much more local level than is usually provided by local news.

Examples:

Yet the *Times*'s entry into the game is an encouraging sign that big players still see a future in hyperlocal coverage, a model that virtually eliminates the huge printing and delivery costs that burden newspaper publishers. —Johnnie L. Roberts, "Peytonplace.com," *Newsweek*, October 3, 2009

As newspapers shutter and traditional media models crumble, the public and private sectors have recognized a need, and perhaps a very lucrative opportunity, to invest in hyperlocal, or community-level, media. —Rachel Sterne, "Making Sense of the Hyperlocal Landscape," *The Huffington Post*, November 12, 2009

The problem so far has been one primarily driven by competition: many towns and local communities have been served by a local community newspaper for years, and while some of the attention has switched online, the switch hasn't been large enough so far to sustain hyperlocal news sites that by their very nature have a limited and small audience constrained by geography. —Duncan Riley, "Hyperlocal Websites Will Boom in 2009 as Community Newspapers Fold," *The Inquisitor*, January 4, 2009

I've mentioned this here many times, the real opportunity in hyperlocal products for news media companies is in aggregating lowcost advertising products in a local version of adwords and offering them in a turnkey online self-service platform to local bloggers. —David Johnson, "Forrester: Is Hyperlocal Hype or Happening?" *Lost Remote*, February 3, 2009

Hyperlocal has the widest currency in journalism and blogging.

61 incentivize

/ (in-sen'tə-vīz,)/

verb

- To provide incentives for; to encourage.

Examples:

Its aim is to "incentivize" — that clunky verb, like much else disagreeable, seems to have been born in the 1960s—with many carrots and sticks many millions of mostly Hispanic people to do this and that and to move here and there. — George F. Will, "Out of What 'Shadows'?" *Newsweek*, June 4, 2007

Sure, we can "incentivize" against the current form of corporate bad behavior, but then we can just sit back and wait for that bad behavior to morph into a new, perhaps more sophisticated form. —Barry Schwartz, "What Work Is and What It Can Be," *The Huffington Post*, March 9, 2010

Despite high salaries and perks, many faculty see overseas teaching as a risky step off the career ladder. Hence Mr.

Goodman's admiration for Carnegie-Mellon and Texas A&M, which he says "incentivize" it, and for NYU's Dr. Sexton, who "is talking about sending every professor and student to Abu Dhabi." —Martha Bayles, "Strangers in a Foreign Land," *The Wall Street Journal*, August 1, 2008

Incentivize is a word many people dislike, as a verb made from the noun *incentive*, which comes from the Latin word *incentivum*, meaning "setting the tune."

62 inflation

/ (in-flā'shən)/

noun

• Undue expansion or elevation; increase beyond the proper or just amount or value: as, *inflation* of trade, currency, or prices; *inflation* of stocks (that is, of the price of stocks).

Examples:
"The primary reason for the decline in inflation is low demand, as the purchasing power of consumers has really gone down drastically," said Wajahat Ali Khan, an analyst at IGI Securities. —"Pakistan Inflation Slows, Bolsters Rate-Cut Hopes," *The Wall Street Journal*, August 10, 2009

We can get a more accurate estimate of the loss of real estate wealth by accounting for the additional loss in value caused by the devaluation of the dollar caused by inflation. —Michael D. Intriligator and R. Kyle Martin, "The Rise and Fall of Artificial Wealth," *The Huffington Post*, August 17, 2009

It has become accepted wisdom in the markets that the economy is enjoying a V-shaped recovery. My view, however, is that the economic recovery will be ephemeral in nature, whereas a real and lasting recovery will, unfortunately, be found in the rate of inflation. —Michael Pento, "Inflation's Coming V-Shaped Recovery," *Forbes*, April 27, 2010

Inflation is the opposite of *deflation*, "a decrease in the general price level, that is, in the nominal cost of goods and services as well as wages."

63   initial public offering
/ (i-nish'əl pub'lik ô'fər-ing) /

noun
- The first offering to members of the public of stock in a company, normally followed by a listing of that stock on a stock exchange.

Examples:
Then, in August 1995, Netscape had the initial public offering for its stock, the beginning of the subsequent Net

IPO boom. —James Fallows, "Billion-Dollar Babies," *The New York Review of Books*, December 16, 1999

The IPO is expected to trigger a $50 million investment from Japanese auto giant Toyota. —Frank Ahrens, "Economy Watch," *The Washington Post*, June 29, 2010

Tesla founder and Chief Executive Elon Musk boasts, "I think the fact that some of the smartest investors in the world have participated in this IPO is a good indication of our future." —Morgan Brennan, "Elon Musk On What's Next for Tesla," *Forbes*, July 5, 2010

Initial public offering (often abbreviated as *IPO*) is also known as *going public*, where a company allows public ownership through their stocks. This is a way for a company to raise money, but is also risky as the value of the company stock can vacillate.

64 innovation
/ (ĭn̬ə-vā'shən)/

noun

1 The act of innovating; the introduction of new things or methods.
2 A novel change in practice or method; something new introduced into established arrangements of any kind; an unwanted or experimental variation.

Examples:

The excuse for this lag in innovation is undoubtedly that 2009 was a tough year to invest in technology. —Brett King, "Banks Are Losing the Customer and Innovation Battle," *The Huffington Post*, April 24, 2010

I recognize that "change," like its conceptual cousin "innovation," is one of the great watchwords of the modern age. —Roger Kimball, "Why I am not pessimistic," *Pajamas Media*, February 14, 2010

Hall's main innovation is to suggest a parallel between Titania and Elizabeth I: a somewhat tendentious idea since Shakespeare's play is a hymn to marital fecundity and Theseus pointedly suggests the rose distilled is happier than that which withers on the "virgin thorn." —Michael Billington, "A Midsummer's Night Dream," *The Guardian*, February 16, 2010

President Obama: The United States, a nation that has always led the way in innovation, is now being outpaced in math and science education. —"Outlandish Crimes, Undetected; How Iranian Hostage Crisis Unfolded; 'Republican Renaissance'," CNN Transcripts, November 4, 2009

Innovation comes from the Latin word innovare, *meaning "to renew."*

65 insider trading
/ (in-sī'dər trād'ing)/

noun

- Buying or selling securities of a publicly held company by a person who has privileged access to information concerning the company's financial condition or plans.

Examples:

Among the things the division looks for are potential indications of insider trading or manipulation of markets through the dissemination of false or misleading information to investors by companies or other market participants. —Floyd Norris, "Nail the Rumor-Mongers," *The New York Times*, April 1, 2008

Tim Power, the former multi-millionaire restaurateur convicted of insider trading, has been spared jail after pleading that he is now "broke, single and unemployable." —Richard Edwards, "Former millionaire restaurateur convicted of insider trading 'broke, single and unemployable'," *Telegraph*, March 2, 2009

The US Securities and Exchange Commission (SEC) charged Mark Cuban today with insider trading stemming from a 2004 sale of stock in an internet company. —"Cuban charged with insider trading over sale of internet company stock," *The Guardian*, November 17, 2008

A grim reminder of Qwest's once-high-flying days has been playing out in Denver's federal court system in recent months. Former CEO Joe Nacchio, found guilty by a jury of illegal insider trading a year ago, has filed an appeal with the U.S. Supreme Court in an attempt to avoid serving a prison term. —W. David Gardner, "Qwest Mulls Selling Its Nationwide Fiber Network," *Information Week*, April 2, 2009

Insider trading is also known as *insider dealing*.

66

intellectual property

/ (in͵tl-ek'cho͞o-əl prop'ər-tē)/

noun

- Any product of someone's intellect that has commercial value, especially copyrighted material, patents, and trademarks.

Examples:

School officials say the specialized biotech programs prepare students to deal with challenges including the ability to navigate complex regulatory and licensing processes as well as the special intellectual-property issues that govern the commercialization of discoveries in the life sciences, said Ruben Henriquez, the director of the Master of Biotechnology Management program at IE in Madrid. —Andrea Chipman,

"How to Attract Money to Fund Biotech Projects," *The Wall Street Journal*, March 27, 2009

Chinese government officials acknowledged that the country should strengthen protection of intellectual property after two days of meetings with Japanese counterparts and representatives from the private sector that wound down here Thursday. —"China Agrees to Step Up Protection of Intellectual Property," *Nikkei*, August 20, 2010

The lawsuit alleges that Airoha has infringed two patents relating to mixed-signal integrated circuits. . . . "We invest heavily in R&D to build our differentiated technology and must vigorously pursue the defense of our intellectual property," said Nestor Ho, general counsel for Silicon Laboratories. —"Silicon Laboratories Asserts Intellectual Property Rights," *Market Watch*, August 16, 2010

Some examples of *intellectual property* include literary or artistic works, business methods, and industrial processes.

67 **junk bond**
/ (jungk bond)/

noun

- A bond (an instrument of debt) that is considered below "investment grade" due to a significant risk of default by the issuer. The interest rate is higher in order to compensate holders for that risk.

Examples:

In retrospect it seems clear that *Liar's Poker* was more accurate about the junk bond economy of the 1980s, because Lewis had worked on the trading floor of Salomon Brothers and got an automatic education in its business realities. —James Fallows, "Billion-Dollar Babies," *The New York Review of Books*, December 16, 1999

Major credit rating agencies have said the U.S. junk bond default rate could reach double digits in 2009. Consumers are spending less, and tight credit markets are making it hard for companies to refinance existing debt or fund day-to-day needs. —"Investment bankers face uncertain landscape," *The New York Times*, January 1, 2009

The approach back then succeeded in sending scores of S&L executives to prison, as well as junk-bond king Michael Milken and business tycoon Charles Keating Jr. —David Head,

"Too Big to Jail? Executives Unscathed as Regulators Let Banks Report Criminal Fraud," *The Huffington Post*, May 3, 2010

Junk of *junk bond* comes from the Middle English word *jonk*, "an old cable or rope," which extended to mean "old refuse from boats or ships," and then to refer to any refuse or cast-off items.

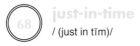

68 **just-in-time**
/ (just in tīm)/

adjective
- Of a manufacturing system in which components are delivered at the precise time required, thus minimizing inventory carrying costs.

Examples:
That goes against the principles of just-in-time production, which dictates holding minimum stocks of raw materials.
—Timothy Aeppel, "Firms Race to Gain Control Over Inventories," *The Wall Street Journal*, February 9, 2009

First, Japan has had huge success in inventory management. The country invented the idea of just-in-time production and delivery, but it has now taken the concept to another new level. —"What Japan Got Right," *Newsweek*, June 12, 2009

He still maintains a full schedule of appearances before every community group under the sun—this is a mayor who not only never stopped campaigning, but runs his administration like the manager of a *just-in-time* retail stocking operation, pushing agency heads to get stuff done almost as soon as the mayor reports back from the neighborhood meetings where residents make demands. —Marc Fisher, "Is Fenty Vulnerable?" *The Washington Post*, June 2, 2009

Just-in-time production uses *kanban*, a Japanese term for "a card containing a set of manufacturing specifications and requirements used to regulate the supply of components; a coordinated manufacturing system using such cards."

69 **kaizen**

/ (kī'zən)/

noun

1 A Japanese business practice of continuous improvement in performance and productivity.
2 Continuous improvement in a general way.

Examples:

The first of 10 commandments of kaizen is "abandon fixed ideas" so that we can all be open to the facts and observed experimental results, rather than our preconceived notions.

—Jon Miller, "The Dirty Secret of Science," *Gemba Panta Rei*, January 17, 2010

Baby Boomers who have been in business are familiar with the Japanese word "kaizen," which when used in the context of Western manufacturing and other industrial and business processes is usually translated as "continuous improvement": Tony Robbins re-badged "kaizen" as CANI—"Continuous And Never-ending Improvement." —Toby Bloomberg, "Diva Marketing Talks Boomers Step Into Social Media With Des Walsh, Barbara Rozgonyi & Carlos Hernandez," *Diva Marketing Blog*, April 9, 2009

Either way, in many plants, lean terms such as kaizen, five-whys and poke-yoke are becoming as much a part of the maintenance lexicon as repair, rebuild and overhaul. —Paul V. Arnold, "On the minds of maintenance," *Reliable Plant*, November 2008

Kaizen is a Japanese term first introduced into English by author Boyé Lafayette De Mente in his book, *Japanese Etiquette and Ethics in Business* (1959).

(70) **kanban**

/ (kän'bän,/)

noun

1 A card containing a set of manufacturing specifications and requirements, used to regulate the supply of components.

2 A coordinated manufacturing system using such cards.

Examples:

What is most interesting is the other motive for the kanban system: the elimination of ledgers. The goal of eliminating paper record keeping was once abandoned due to requirements by Japanese tax authorities. When computers were introduced into the offices in the early 1950s and the elimination of the ledgers was finally allowed by the tax authorities, the kanban system finally became possible. —Jon Miller, "Excerpts from an Interview with Taiichi Ohno, July 16, 1984," *Gemba Panta Rei*, February 16, 2010

In a continuous flow system, features are pulled from the backlog and then worked on continuously until they are completed. If there are identifiable stages during development, a kanban board can be used to identify where work in progress is stacking up. These bottlenecks are then targeted for process improvement, to keep the work flowing through

the system efficiently. —Chris Sims, "Are Kanban Workflows Agile?"
Info Q, April 6, 2009

Kanban is a Japanese term, literally meaning "visible board," and
is used in *just-in-time production*, "a manufacturing system in which
components are delivered at the precise time required, thus minimizing inventory carrying costs."

71 **key performance indicator**
/ (kē pər-fôr'məns in'di-kā‚tər)/

noun
- A financial or nonfinancial metric used to help an organization define and measure progress toward organizational
  goals.

Examples:
Datuk Seri Najib Tun Razak has introduced a comprehen-
sive key performance indicator (KPI) to gauge the performance and achievements of his cabinet to symbolise the
reform and approach of a more responsible, focused and
people-centric government. —"Najib to review ministers' performance every 6 months," *My Sinchew*, April 9, 2009

Research reveals that a lack of insight as to how to convert
key performance indicator/metric reporting into actionable
strategy is the top frustration end-users experience, whether

they leverage a free solution, a paid solution, or both. —Alex Jefferies, "Drowning in Data: Web Analytics and Information Overload," *CRM Buyer*, April 16, 2009

While inventory turns is the main KPI for evaluating supply chain agility, logistics cost KPI allow firms to evaluate the efficiency of their logistics and SCM operations. —"Logistics and Supply Chain Management (SCM)," *BNET*, October 2006

Protection of "sacrosanct" rights is not, and has never been, an important KPI. —Tom Doctoroff, "Human Rights in China: What Consumer Behavior Reveals," *The Huffington Post*, February 27, 2009

Within each *key performance indicator* (often abbreviated as *KPI*), a company may establish a *benchmark*, "a standard by which something"—in this case, success—"is evaluated or measured."

72   labor union

/ (lā'bər yōōn'yən)/

noun

- A continuous association of wage earners for the purpose of maintaining or improving the conditions of their employment; a trade union.

Examples:

A. Philip Randolph took over the Brotherhood of Sleeping Car Porters in 1925 and made it into an organization of historical importance far beyond its numbers. Randolph turned a labor union into a freedom movement, and during its twelve-year battle with the Pullman Company to become the first black union recognized by a major US corporation, he helped to transform attitudes among blacks toward unions, toward themselves as workers, and to end organized labor's antagonism toward black workers. —Darryl Pinckney, "Keeping the Faith," *The New York Review of Books*, November 22, 1990

Labor experts believe the party's leaders are very concerned about a scenario like that in Poland in the late 1980s in which an independent labor-union movement led to the overthrow of the Polish government and contributed to the dismantling of the entire Eastern bloc under the Soviet Union. —Norihiko Shirouzo, "Chinese Workers Challenge Beijing's Authority," *The Wall Street Journal*, June 13, 2010

One afternoon last week, dozens of Hanabusa's labor-union supporters waved signs in the rain for nearly two hours until the candidate arrived. —Philip Rucker, "In Hawaii, intraparty feud may cost Democrats a seat in Congress," *The Washington Post*, May 7, 2010

A *labor union* is known as a *trade union* in British English, and is sometimes referred to simply as a *union*.

73

launch
/ (lônch *or* länch)/

verb
- To send out; to start (one) on a career; to set going; to give a start to (something); to put in operation.

noun
- The act of launching.

Examples:

"This launch is a big one for us," says Sanjay Purohit, marketing director for Cadbury's candy in India. —Deborah Ball, "Cadbury's New Bubble-Gum Battle," *The Wall Street Journal*, October 4, 2007

Monday night PEPS and the Family Center of South Snohomish County held a launch party to mark the program's debut in Snohomish County. —Pat Ratliff, "Being a better parent starts with PEPS," *Edmonds Beacon*, October 9, 2008

Among other carrots to draw viewers at the beta launch is the availability of every episode from all six seasons of "The Sopranos," along with such contemporary movies as "Slumdog Millionaire," "Milk" and the first two "Chronicles of Narnia" pics. —Cynthia Littleton, "Comcast Unveils Video Service," *Variety*, December 15, 2009

Launch comes from the Latin word *lanceare*, meaning "to wield a lance."

(74) **level-set**
/ (lev'əl set)/

noun
- A state of mutual understanding among parties.

verb
- To establish a baseline of mutual understanding.

Examples:

"We asked people to identify areas where they think they are the best and where they have the biggest areas for improvement," he says. "Representatives from across the country will look at these 'best practices' and say, yes or no. If it is a best practice, it's my responsibility to get that implemented at our Seattle plants." On-site maintenance training through Clemson will not only work to solidify and push these practices down the command chain, but also will work to level-set the language between plants. —Paul V. Arnold, "Boeing: Taking Flight," *Reliable Plant*, March 2008

The next steps—to try to "race ahead"—are to add focused high-speed Internet and phone services that bring in customers and keep them, as they do with the general population. "I think the bundle definitely helps level-set for us," Polk said. —Kent Gibbons, "Cable Show 2010: Operator Exploits Multicultural Edges," *Multichannel News*, May 1, 2010

The original meaning of *level set* is mathematical: "the set of values x for which a real-valued function $f(x)$ is equal to a given constant."

75 leverage

/ (lev'ər-ij *or* lē'vər-)/

noun

1. The use of borrowed funds with a contractually determined return to increase the ability of a business to invest and earn an expected higher return, but usually at high risk.
2. Any influence that is compounded or used to gain an advantage.
3. The ability to earn very high returns when operating at a high capacity utilization of a facility.

verb

- To use; to exploit; to take full advantage (of something).

Examples:

Leverage refers to how much money you've borrowed compared with the capital you have on hand. Let's say you're buying a house, and you put 20 percent down. Your leverage is 5:1. For every dollar you had in capital, you've borrowed four more to complete the sale. —Ezra Klein, "Explaining financial regulation: Leverage and capital requirements," *The Washington Post*, April 19, 2010

The House and Senate Judiciary Committees authorized the Democratic chairmen to subpoena Karl Rove and others. Now, they haven't decided to issue those subpoenas yet. Instead, Democrats call it leverage—a bargaining chip in the hope of negotiating a compromise with the White House. Republicans argued it was premature. —"Illegal Alien Amnesty; Addiction and School Children; Attorney Firings Issues," CNN Transcripts, March 24, 2007

Leverage comes from the Middle English word *lever,* meaning "to raise."

76 long tail

/ (long tāl *or* long tāl) /

noun

- Sales made for less usual goods within a very large choice, which can return a profit through reduced marketing and distribution costs. Also *long-tail.*

Examples:
Meanwhile [Amazon.com CEO Jeff Bezos] sees dust gathering on oldschool print publishers while more and more

writers short-circuit the submission process and follow up self-publishing with long-tail Internet marketing as though they were Indie bands mixing new tunes. —Giles Slade, "Impulse Buying for Books, Baby," *The Huffington Post*, February 10, 2009

The long-tail hypotheses, whereby specialized applications and content are profitably delivered to ever smaller customer segments, continues to prove elusive. —Michael I. Morgenstern, "Open Versus Shut Approaches to Building Business," *The Wall Street Journal*, June 1, 2010

The average consumer does not need 225,000 apps. He or she needs the top 50; everything else is just long-tail noise. —Ron Adner and William Vincent, "BlackBerry's Next Killer App," *Forbes*, June 18, 2010

An example of a business that follows the *long tail* selling model is Amazon.com, which sells a huge variety of goods, although they may only sell a few of each.

77 **macroeconomics**
/ (mak̩rō-ek̩ə-nom'iks *or* mak̩rō ē̩kə nom'iks)/

noun

• The study of the entire economy in terms of the total amount of goods and services produced, total income earned, the level of employment of productive resources, and the general behavior of prices.

Examples:

First, companies rely on macroeconomic forecasting in their strategic planning and budgeting and for gaining insight about customers and competitors. And macroeconomic theory underlies much of government policymaking. —"The Future of Economic Forecasting," *Forbes*, November 18, 2009

This is as close to a "scientific experiment" as there can be in macroeconomics: from '33 to '36 Roosevelt unleashed the New Deal and what passed at the time as massive spending. —Paul Abrams, "Winning the Economic Argument: Show Opponents This Graph, and Ask Them to Explain," *The Huffington Post*, February 16, 2009

Yet, while perhaps a few people enjoy studying economic principles for their own sake, the main reason anyone would study macroeconomics is to try to understand how we—as a society, nation, and world—can reach the goals we desire . . . . In the context of macroeconomics, we can say that three

especially important components of well-being are: good living standards; stability and security; and sustainability.
—Frank Ackerman, Julie A. Nelson, and Thomas Weisskopf, "Macroeconomic goals," *The Encyclopedia of Earth*, October 22, 2007

The *macro* in *macroeconomics* comes from the Greek word *makros*, meaning "long, large."

78 mentor
/ (men'tər)/

noun
- One who acts as a wise and faithful guide and monitor, especially of a younger person; an intimate friend who is also a sage counselor, especially to someone who is young or inexperienced.

verb
- To act as someone's mentor.

Examples:
Cucayo participants such as Claudia Landivar, who came back from Spain to start a cosmetics business, say the guidance from the mentor is as important as the grant money. —
Matt Moffett and Jonathan House, "Spanish Downturn Sparks Immigrant Exodus," *The Wall Street Journal*, July 1, 2010

However, for women at all rungs of the ladder, finding a mentor is a daunting process that is rarely, if ever, demystified. —Hannah Seligson, "Even Tiger Woods Has a Coach. So Should You," *The Huffington Post*, January 22, 2007

Some disciples may feel that the mentor is the only one who understands them and thus fall in love. —Alexander Berzin, *Relating to a Spiritual Teacher: Building a Healthy Relationship*, 2000

The job of a mentor is a simple one—make reading fun, according to Trisha Huebner, program director in Rutland for the past three years. —Cristina Kumka, "Learning to love books: One student at a time," *Rutland Herald*, November 23, 2009

In Greek mythology, a character named *Mentor* was the trusted counselor of Odysseus, the king of Ithaca and a leader in the Trojan War.

79 **microeconomics**

/ (mī͜krō-ek͜ə-nom'iks *or* mī͜krō -ēk͜ə-nom'iks)/

noun

- The field of economics that deals with small-scale economic activities such as those of the individual or company.

Examples:

A true believer in microeconomics, Mr. Jordan hopes that consumers will take a stand by making better choices to drive less, conserve energy, carpool, and take public transportation, if available. —Angie Santiago, "N.C. Contradictions: Mapping General Election Territory," *The Huffington Post*, May 7, 2008

The success of Freakonomics and similar books tell their own story: until the crisis broke in 2007, it was assumed that the big picture was largely sorted and economists needed to concentrate on micro-economics, where much good work has been done, incidentally. —Larry Elliott, "It's a funny old game: where is the dream team of economists to tackle the slump?" *The Guardian*, June 1, 2009

Daly shows how traditional marginal analysis in microeconomics, which fails to internalize environmental and social externalities, will lead to overestimation of macroeconomic gross national product (GNP). —Mohan Munasinghe, "Restructuring development and growth for greater sustainability," *The Encyclopedia of Earth*, July 22, 2009

I was friendly with the owners of an Exxon station in Virginia Beach, and they explained the micro-economics of their business to me. They went over their books and showed me that they didn't set the gas prices, although they had to factor in their needs by adding pennies to the higher prices per gallon to stay afloat. —Peter Galuszka, "Who a BP boycott hits hardest," *The Washington Post*, June 10, 2010

The *micro* of *microeconomics* comes from the Greek word *mikros*, meaning "small."

80 mindshare
/ (mīnd shâr)/

noun

- A consumer's awareness of a particular brand or product compared to that of its rivals.

Examples:
But it's no wonder why they took to the airwaves right as Bing was making its big publicity push: With fickle user bases that can switch to competing software with the flick of a mouse, mindshare is becoming almost as important to tech companies as it is to celebrities. —Ryan Tate, "Microsoft's Bing Puts Google and Yahoo on the Defensive," *Valleywag*, June 10, 2009

If Microsoft or Yahoo! or a startup search engine wants to take market share, they're going to have to think less like a technology company trying to build a better mousetrap and more like a brand trying to win mindshare from a beloved competitor. —"Struggling Against Google's Greatest Advantage," *SEOmoz*, January 26, 2009

In stock market terms, developer mindshare is one of the hottest "commodities" in the mobile business, one whose "stock price" has ballooned in the last two years. —Kui Kinyanjui, "'Techpreneurs' Find Niche in Development of Phone Software," *All Africa*, July 22, 2010

Mindshare is a play on *market share,* the "percentage of some market held by a company."

mission statement
/ (mish'ən stāt'mənt)/

noun

- A declaration of the overall goal or purpose of an organization.

Examples:

Unite your values, standards and character into your mission statement as a way of communicating your strategy to your employees, contractors and business associates. —Kim Beasley, "Your Business Mission Statement," *Every Joe*, June 24, 2009

As Klara Sax, an artist, watches the ending, she muses: "All Eisenstein wants you to see, in the end, are the contradictions of being." . . . That might serve as a mission statement for the novel. —Luc Sante, "Between Hell and History," *The New York Review of Books*, November 6, 1997

The construction of a mission statement or a strategic plan is in some ways an open invitation to dissemble, pander and obfuscate. —"Integrity," *Stanford Encyclopedia of Philosophy*, August 10, 2008

A growing number of multimillionaires and billionaires, hoping to stave off costly feuds, are drawing up family mission statements—lofty treatises filled with words like "legacy," "values" and "stewardship" that aim to carry rich families (and their fortunes) safely through the ages. —Robert Frank, "New Status Symbol: Family Mission Statements," *The Wall Street Journal*, October 12, 2007

A type of *mission statement* is a *vision statement,* a declaration issued by a company or organization in which its intentions for the future are stated.

82 **monetize**
/ (mon'i-tīz, *or* mun'-)/

verb

- To be able to realize revenue for a product or service, especially one that was previously provided free of charge.

Examples:
What has really struck me over the years now is the fact that media companies have looked at the Internet as either a dis-

traction, or in some cases a threat, but not as the giant opportunity that it is. It's challenging obviously because with the business models, the ability to monetize is not always evident. —"Susan Lyne's Digital Makeover," *Newsweek*, July 9, 2009

By late 2008, YouTube's attempts to "monetize" its vast streams of amateur videos had hit choppy water. —Dan Schiller and Christian Sandvig, "Is YouTube the Successor to Televsion–or to LIFE Magazine?" *The Huffington Post*, March 12, 2010

To him, the culprit for Facebook's struggle to successfully monetize is simply because on Facebook, he said, "people are more excited about their friends than they are about my brand." —Jessica Tsai, "Retailers Better Buy in to Social Media," *CRM Magazine*, February 27, 2009

Sure, it's all fun and cool, but when there's no return on your investment . . . it soon becomes clear that the ability to "monetize"–i.e., make some money or at least compensate for the time spent–is still the one thing that everyone, from the old-media moguls to the new-media mavens, is still trying to discover. —Belinda Acosta, "Follow the Leader," *The Austin Chronicle*, May 15, 2009

Monetize is another example of a noun turned into a verb.

83 **monopoly**
/ (mə-nop'ə-lē)/

noun

1 A situation, by legal privilege or other agreement, in which solely one party (company, cartel, etc.) exclusively provides a particular product or service, dominating that market and generally exerting powerful control over it.
2 An exclusive control over the trade or production of a commodity or service through exclusive possession.
3 The market thus controlled.

Examples:

Second, the concentration of all the productive industries, except agriculture, into great establishments, while it has enormously lessened the cost of production, has so reduced the number of competing units that a monopoly is the inevitable final result. —Charles Whiting Baker, *Monopolies and the People*, 1889

Monopolies are one example of capitalism failing. Monopolies have virtually no competition and can dictate prices to their customers unless they are restricted by regulators. The customer either has to pay the price demanded by the monopoly or not receive that good/service. —Howard Steve Friedman, "When Capitalism Fails–The Ugly World of Monopolies," *The Huffington Post*, June 24, 2010

Monopoly comes from the Greek word *monopōlion*—a blend of *monos*, meaning "single, alone," plus *pōlein*, meaning "to sell."

84 **mortgage**

/ (môr'gij)/

noun

- A special form of secured loan where the purpose of the loan must be specified to the lender, to purchase assets that must be fixed (not movable) property, such as a house or piece of farmland. The assets are registered as the legal property of the borrower but the lender can seize them and dispose of them if they are not satisfied with the manner in which the repayment of the loan is conducted by the borrower. Once the loan is fully re-paid, the lender loses this right of seizure and the assets are then deemed to be unencumbered.

verb

- As in "to *mortgage* a property," to borrow against a prop-erty, to obtain a loan for another purpose by giving away the right of seizure to the lender over a fixed property, such as a house or piece of land.

Examples:

But your mortgage is a business deal, and it is not immoral to walk away from a business deal unless you went in to the deal with the intention of defaulting. —Dylan Ratigan, "They Keep Stealing—Why Keep Paying?" *The Huffington Post*, June 24, 2010

If he fails to make payments on the mortgage, your credit will be hurt. If your relationship ends, you won't be able to get your name off the mortgage unless he refinances the home. —Ilyce R. Glink and Samuel J. Tamkin, "Real estate matters: Clarifying long-term homeowner tax credit eligibility," *The Washington Post*, May 8, 2010

Mortgage comes from the Old French word *mort*, meaning "dead" plus *gage*, meaning "pledge."

85 network effect
/ (net'wûrk i-fekt')/

noun
- The higher growth rate of businesses with higher market share in those segments of the economy in which the value of a product or a service depends on the number of existing users of the product or a service, as is the case with telephone networks.

Examples:
[Skype] has single-handedly altered the business of communications, and I believe that its business model is exactly what it needs to be. Having amassed a huge user base, it is

a fortunate beneficiary of the inverse network effect theory (which dictates that it should resist opening its network except in the most limited and controlled ways). —Eric Hernaez, "Skype: Not Open Enough," *TMC Net Bloggers*, January 2, 2009

However, he remains optimistic: "Venture capital was a network-effect business where good returns breed good returns and new funds and good entrepreneurs attract good entrepreneurs." —James Mawsom, "All European Roads Lead Back to Skype," *The Wall Street Journal*, August 25, 2009

Even though public transport is a classic example of a network effect and the Luas is in fact good for bus services Mr. Lynch appears to think that other providers are the competition he needs to worry about. —David Rolfe, "Dublin Bus: Get people out of their cars? We compete against the Luas!" *Rolfe's Random Review*, February 3, 2009

Online social networks are dependent upon the *network effect*—the existence of users—for their success.

86 oligopoly

/ (ol̩i-gop'ə-lē *or* ō̩li-gop'ə-lē)/

noun

- An economic condition in which a small number of sellers exert control over the market of a commodity.

Examples:

In oligopoly competition situations, prices move in lock step, even without overt (and illegal!) collusion between the parties. There is simply no force in the system to get the price to stop at the equilibrium between supply and demand. Adam Smith's "invisible hand" is totally absent from this kind of market. —Dr. Philip Neches, "Then There Were Three," *The Huffington Post*, May 3, 2010

An oligopoly is when only a small number of large vendors sell a product or service. Oligopolies can occur naturally, when a company creates a great product and captures most of the market. But they are often a result of government policies that favor some players over others by restricting or eliminating competition, which often leads to higher prices and lower quality. —Merrill Matthews, "America's Coming Health Care Oligopoly," *Forbes*, July 7, 2010

But we also know, as believers in free enterprise, that the only real way to "reform" an oligopoly is to eliminate it. —Steven Bavaria, "Competition Key to Better Ratings," *The Wall Street Journal*, July 5, 2008

Oligopoly comes from the Greek word *oligos*, meaning "few," plus *pōlien*, meaning "to sell."

87 **outsource**

/ (out'sôrs, *or* out'sōrs,)/

verb

- To transfer the management and/or day-to-day execution of an entire business function to a third-party service provider.

Examples:

And Taiwan has been very creative in the way they have organized their economy. They invented the business model that has come to dominate semiconductor production, the "foundry" model in which designers and inventors of semiconductors out-source the actual manufacturing to third party foundries like those in Taiwan. —Gilbert B. Kaplan, "Letter from Taiwan: 100 Million Manufacturing Employees Next Door," *The Huffington Post*, December 29, 2009

In previous times—in Britain at any rate—one could manage quite nicely by letting Harrods do some of the work. A display advertisement for the store in July 1919 was reassuring to those who wanted (and could afford) to out-source the difficulty. —"Holiday Catering," *The Old Foodie*, March 19, 2010

Rather than fixing the problems and hiring people who understand the system counties appear ready to out-source

our elections. —John Gideon, "'Daily Voting News' for June 3, 2008,"
OpEdNews.com, July 3, 2008

The sense of *source* in *outsource* is "to obtain or procure; used especially of a business resource."

88 / (ō'vər thə koun'tər) /

adjective

- Direct interaction between two parties without an intermediary. Thus, any market where items such as stocks or currency are bought and sold at a distance, rather than on the exchange.

Examples:
But in over-the-counter (OTC) markets—in which parties trade privately with each other rather than through a centralized exchange—it is not at all transparent what other deals are being done. —Viral V. Acharya and Robert Engle, "Derivatives Trades Should All Be Transparent," *The Wall Street Journal*, May 15, 2009

Though Mr. Madoff told some investors he did his options trading in the over-the-counter market, analysts question that account as well. —Aaron Lucchetti, Amir Efrati, and Tom Lauricella, "Madoff's Point Man Is Cast in Same Role for Prosecutors," *The Wall Street Journal*, January 21, 2009

Much more exacting regulation of credit derivatives, including opening up large parts of the over the counter market to full public disclosure and scrutiny, now seems inevitable, which will in turn substantially affect margins and returns.
—Jeremy Warner, "Goldman Sachs changes mark end of era," *Telegraph*, April 19, 2010

Over-the-counter (abbreviated as *OTC*) also refers to medicine or other treatments "legal for sale or distribution without the requirement of a prescription."

89 paradigm
/ (par'ə-dīm, *or* par'ə -dim,)/

noun
1 An example serving as a model or pattern.
2 A system of assumptions, concepts, values, and practices that constitutes a way of viewing reality.

Examples:
A "paradigm" is a whole "worldview" or "explanatory framework," and individual scientists can have "vested interests" in a paradigm—but scientists also have a strong vested interest in coming up with new paradigms. —Phillip Ellis Jackson,

"The Politics of Science and Religion: Part II," *Intellectual Conservative*, April 20, 2009

The shift in paradigm is supposed to open computing to the next billion people because PCs (or better yet netbooks) would be simpler and cheaper, built, perhaps, around a species of Google's own Linux-based Android operating system and Chrome browser. —Maureen O'Gara, "Google GDrive: Supposedly Where the Rubber Meets the Road," *Web 2.0 Journal*, January 28, 2009

A *paradigm shift* is "a radical change in thinking from an accepted point of view to a new belief."

90 **patent**

/ (pat'nt)/

noun

- A declaration issued by a government agency declaring someone the inventor of a new invention and having the privilege of stopping others from making, using, or selling the claimed invention; a letter patent.

verb

- To successfully register an invention with a government agency; to secure a letter patent.

Examples:

For instance, in 1857, a Negro slave, living with his master in the state of Mississippi, perfected a valuable invention which his master sought to have protected by a patent. Now, in law, a patent is a contract between the government and the inventor or his assignees. The slave, although the inventor, could not under the law be a party to a contract, and therefore could not secure the patent himself. —Daniel Wallace Culp, *Twentieth Century Negro Literature*, 1902

In a suit against the Boston Incandescent Lamp Company et al., in the United States Circuit Court for the District of Massachusetts, decided in favor of Edison on June 11, 1894, Judge Colt, in his opinion, said, among other things: "Edison made an important invention; he produced the first practical incandescent electric lamp; the patent is a pioneer in the sense of the patent law; it may be said that his invention created the art of incandescent electric lighting." —Frank Lewis Dyer and Thomas Commerford Martin, *Edison, His Life and Inventions*, 1910

Patent comes from and is short for the Old French phrase *lettre patente*, meaning "open letter."

91 **piggyback**
/ (pig'ē-bak,)/

adverb
- On somebody's back or shoulders.

verb
- To attach or append something to another (usually larger) object or event.

Examples:
Consent letters will be used to give the affected residents, from whom the "employee portion" of FICA tax was withheld and paid over to the IRS, notice of their opportunity to "piggyback" on the teaching hospital's efforts to obtain a refund of the teaching hospital's "employer-portion" of FICA tax. —David Ivill, Ira Mirsky, and Thomas Borders, "Teaching Hospitals, Ex-Residents, in Line for Billions in Tax Refunds," *Forbes*, April 13, 2010

The study concluded the services like these "pose an operational challenge to telcos as they 'piggyback' on the existing communications infrastructure, imposing network capacity issues and increased costs for the network providers." —Art Brodsky, "Will Social Media Be Tweeted, Facebooked and MySpaced—Or Squashed?" *The Huffington Post*, March 15, 2009

Lenders also extended more "second-lien" mortgages—many of them "piggyback" second loans that borrowers used to cover down payments. —Rick Brooks and Constance Mitchell Ford, "The United States of Subprime," *The Wall Street Journal*, October 11, 2007

Piggyback may be an alteration of *pickback*, *pick* being an alteration of *pitch*, meaning "throw."

92   pilot

/ (pī'lət)/

adjective

- Made or used as a test or demonstration of capability (e.g., *pilot* run, *pilot* plant).

verb

- To test or have a preliminary trial of (an idea, a new product, etc.).

Examples:

Two cable powerhouses announced an ambitious pilot program Wednesday that aims to convince their customers that, actually, TV on the web should not be free. —Eliot Van Buskirk, "Time Warner, Comcast Depart From Hulu Model With 'TV Everywhere'," *Wired*, June 24, 2009

During a six-week pilot run in Southampton and Basing-stoke, more than 500 appointments were given to members of the public who had been victims of burglary, theft, threats and assaults, or anti-social behaviour. —"PCs by appointment," *Isle of Wight County Press*, April 6, 2009

Last year it launched a pilot product called the Contributory Plan, with a goal of signing up 100 small businesses. — Julie M. Donnelly, "Express delivery: Connector unveils health insurance," *Boston Business Journal*, March 12, 2010

Pilot comes from the Greek word *pēda*, meaning "steering oar."

(93) Ponzi scheme
/ (pon'zē skēm)/

noun
- A fraudulent scheme where earlier investors are paid with the money taken from new investors, giving the impression that the scheme is a viable investment.

Examples:
His polemic peaks in this line: "The GDR [East Germany] was a Ponzi scheme that fell in a bank run.". . . But a state is not a bank, let alone a Ponzi scheme. States can live for long periods with large debt burdens. States do not simply

"go bankrupt." —Timonthy Garton Ash, "1989," *The New York Review of Books*, November 5, 2009

After being accused of running a Ponzi scheme that duped more than 100 investors out of $12 million, after running from the police, and after a failed suicide attempt, Hernandez' wife is bringing more bad news to the accused criminal. Gina Hernandez may be serving up divorce papers to him soon and, unlike her husband, she isn't trying to fool anyone. —Tara Grimes, "Con Man's Wife Dishes Up More Bad News," *NBC Chicago*, June 24, 2009

Because of the size of Mr. Madoff's money-management business, some have speculated that he had help in orchestrating what he described as a Ponzi scheme. —Kara Scannell and Nathan Koppel, "Broad Probe into Hedge Fund," *The Wall Street Journal*, December 26, 2008

Ponzi scheme is named after Charles *Ponzi*, an early twentieth-century speculator who organized such a scheme.

postmortem

/ (pōst-môr'təm)/

noun

- Any investigation occurring after something considered unsuccessful, especially used of meetings, bridge games, and software development.

Examples:

A post-mortem, in the medical sense, is when you carve up a body to figure out why it died. But the term has migrated into the patois of American business, where (in corporate terms) a post-mortem is a meeting held after the completion of a project, where you review the course of the project from beginning to end. You look at what went right, and what went wrong, and then you try to improve the procedure for future projects, in an effort to avoid making the same mistakes over again. —Chris Weigant, "Health Reform Post-Mortem," *The Huffington Post*, March 22, 2010

If and when an honest postmortem is completed, the results will demonstrate that the Grand Old Party, as it once deserved to be known, was responsible for the worst excesses, with very few exceptions. —Joe Conason, "G.O.P. Campaign Tactics Reveal True Character," *The New York Observer*, November 12, 2006

According to this postmortem from the Dcortesi blog, the attacks exploited gaping holes that allowed users to insert tags in the URLs of Twitter users' profile pages that called malicious javascript from third-party web servers. —Dan Goodin, "Twitter overrun by weekend of powerful worm attacks," *The Register*, April 13, 2009

Postmortem comes from the Latin word *post*, meaning "afterward" plus *mors*, meaning "death."

95 proactive

/ (prō ak'tiv)/

adjective
- Acting in advance to deal with an expected change or difficulty.

Examples:
Now, let's talk prevention—or as I prefer to call it "proactive health care." To me, "prevention" implies a defensive posture of warding off disease, while "proactive" empowers us to address problems ahead of the curve when it's easier and cheaper to do so, rather than down-line when disease progression makes it more expensive. —Alison Rose Levy, "The Power of Prevention," *The Huffington Post*, June 30, 2009

UBS credit analyst Fumihito Gotoh notes that "the reasons why Japan's corporate sector's funding demand is sluggish include delays in proactive overseas expansion, the social trend in the post-high growth era not strongly advocating entrepreneurship, and management's insufficient understanding of 'cost of capital' (most corporate management thinks that debt is a vice)." —Takuji Aida, "Saving Japan from Corporate Savings," *The Wall Street Journal*, August 9, 2010

We all outgrow our jobs eventually, but being proactive is the key to emerging from it a victor, and not a victim.
—Carolyn McFann, "Kicking that Ungrateful Employer to the Curb and Moving to a Better Job," *Ground Report*, October 20, 2007

Proactive is the opposite of *reactive*, "reacting or responding to a stimulus; reacting to the past rather than anticipating the future, not predictive."

96

prosumer
/ (prō-soō'mər)/

noun

1 A person in postindustrial society who combines the economic roles of producer and consumer.

2 A serious, enthusiastic consumer: not professional (earning money), but of similar interest and skills to a (gen-

erally lower level) professional, or aspiring to such. The target market of prosumer equipment.

adjective

1 A product targeted at serious, enthusiastic consumers, incorporating professional features but often modified for non-professional use.
2 A high-end consumer product more generally.

Examples:

Such cameras have been around for years but were generally priced only for serious professionals; now, however, such models are dropping closer to the "prosumer" range of $1000-plus. —"Practical Futurist: What's Next for Digital Photography," *Newsweek*, July 22, 2003

And second, many of those youths are already active "prosumers" of news: people who not only digest news but also document the world around them, both to get the word out about what they eyewitness, as well as to call attention to injustices they see. —Susan Moeller, "Media Literacy 101: Of Toilets, UNESCO and Demand-Side News," *The Huffington Post*, September 22, 2009

Depending on the context, *prosumer* is a blend of the words *producer* and *consumer*, with the idea that consumers would take on the role of mass customization, or of *professional* and *consumer*, referring to serious amateur enthusiasts.

97 pushback

/ (poosh'bak,)/

noun

- Backlash of any sort; the act of repelling such as an enemy; criticism of or resistance to a proposal, stance, or event.

Examples:

The goal of this kind of pushback is to discredit the Times reporting on a possible sex scandal, thereby discounting the entire story of corruption, reminiscent to the destruction of Dan Rather's reporting on George W. Bush's time in the Texas Air National Guard. —Matt Browner Hamlin, "McCain's Non-Denial Denial of an Intervention," *The Huffington Post*, February 21, 2008

Beyond that, a strong pushback is emerging on the left wing of President Barack Obama's Democratic party, whose denizens argue it's wrongheaded to focus on fighting deficits right now, when the recovery is stumbling and in need of additional juice from government spending. —Gerald F. Seib, "Tapping Reagan's Growth Theme," *The Wall Street Journal*, July 6, 2010

Remember, we have don't ask don't tell in the first place because of the intense pushback from the military on President Clinton's move in 1993 to fulfill his promise to end the ban. —Jonathan Capeheart, "Justified anger over Sec. Gates' letter on don't ask don't tell," *The Washington Post*, May 4, 2010

Pushback originated as a military term, as opposed to *pullback,* "the act or result of pulling back; a withdrawal."

98 **pyramid scheme**
/ (pir'ə-mid skēm)/

noun
- An illicit moneymaking investment scheme whereby early investors are paid primarily or wholly by later investors. Eventually all such schemes fail to the detriment of recent (later) investors.

Examples:
The company arrived in 1995 and quickly drew the ire of the government, which was frightened by an Amway sales culture that inspired almost fanatic devotion. . . . Meanwhile, economic reforms had spawned dozens of pyramid-scheme scandals the government was frantically trying to eradicate. —Dan Levin, "Amway's China Redux," *Forbes*, August 27, 2009

While accusing the church of weirdness, pyramid-scheme-like financing, and, worst of all, bad aesthetics, I did say that much of what makes us uncomfortable about Scientology is that its crimes are exaggerated versions of our own. For example, Scientology does charge for services, but Mormons are expected to tithe 10 percent, and Protestant preachers have been known to bar the doors until the collection plates fill up to a healthier level. —Mark Oppenheimer, "Jenna Elfman, Will You Be My Scientologist Friend?" *The Huffington Post*, August 2, 2007

Pyramid schemes are a type of *fraud*, "an artifice employed by one person for the purpose of deceiving another, to the prejudice of his right; the causing or making use of the error of another for the attainment of an illegal object."

99 quality assurance
/ (kwol'i-tē ə-shoor'əns)/

noun

- A system in which the delivery of a service or the quality of a product is assessed, and compared with that required. Often abbreviated QA.

Examples:
As services pervade how and what IT delivers, quality assurance early and often becomes the gatekeeper of suc-

cess—or the points of failure. —Dana Gardner, "Service Integrity Supports Cloud Computing," *JDJ*, June 24, 2009

The [College of American Pathologists] is widely considered the leader in laboratory quality assurance and is an advocate for high-quality and cost-effective medical care. —"FAMC departments awarded accreditation," *Fremont Tribune*, June 24, 2009

Use evidence of quality provided by acknowledged competent authorities on academic quality such as recognized accreditation and quality assurance bodies. —"CHEA and UNESCO Issue Statement on Effective Practice to Discourage Degree Mills," *Los Angeles Chronicle*, June 24, 2009

With drives being as cheap as they are, you know that the manufacturers can't spend a ton of effort in QA and test on each device. —Leo Notenboom, "How long should a hard drive last?" *Ask Leo!* July 24, 2010

Quality assurance is similar to *quality control*, "a control, such as inspection or testing, introduced into an industrial or business process to ensure quality."

100 recession
/ (ri-sesh'ən)/

noun

* A period of reduced economic activity.

Examples:
The simple lesson when you are deep in recession is that a serious policy error is to reverse stimulus too early, which then sends the economy crashing into a depression. —Mark Bathgate, "Deconstructing David Branchflower," *Spectator*, October 13, 2009

The U.S. economy, if not already in recession, is on the brink, with consumers retrenching. —James B. Stewart, "A Patient Wager on Ford Shows Import of Conviction," *The Wall Street Journal*, April 30, 2008

The two things that are really driving the ascendancy of English as the world's default language now are the global economy, which even in recession is clearly on a different scale than ever before, and the technological revolution of the World Wide Web. —Vit Wagner, "Parlez-vous Globish?" *The Star*, June 11, 2010

Just how long a weak dollar can support prices, with the economy still in recession, is questionable. Crude in storage remains near record highs and demand in the U.S., the world's largest consumer of oil, is sluggish. —John Porretto, "Crude passes $70 but gas prices flatten," *Chicago Defender*, June 9, 2009

A *recession* is the opposite of a *boom*, "a period of prosperity or high market activity."

101 retention
/ (ri-ten'shən)/

noun
* The act of retaining or holding as one's own; continued possession or ownership. In business, the practice of reducing employee turnover or customer churn.

Examples:
DePaolo, who took home $1.7 million in cash and stock last year, says there are years when some of his best lieutenants earn more than he does. Pay is based on such performance measures as the profitability of accounts and customer retention. —Daniel Fisher, "What It Takes to Run a Sound Commercial Bank," *Forbes*, August 26, 2010

Campaigning by the judge, whose retention is being considered, is prohibited except under exceptional circumstances. —Christopher Brauchli, "Money vs. Judicial Merit Selection," *The Huffington Post*, June 10, 2010

AIG also budgeted $57 million in "retention" pay to employees who had left the company, according to a March 2 filing to the Securities and Exchange Commission. —Laura Litvan and Christopher Stern, "AIG Firestorm Has Democrats Edge About Geithner, Team," *Bloomberg*, March 19, 2009

A company hopes to achieve *employee retention,* or ensuring that employees do not leave, by providing benefits and incentives.

102   **rightsize**

/ (rīt sīz)/

verb

- A euphemism for *downsize,* meaning "to reduce in size or number; to reduce the workforce of; to terminate the employment of."

Examples:

But while trimming headcount to "rightsize" a company for its potential markets is a good move in theory, some investors wonder whether the employee reduction may be going too far in some areas, leaving the company at risk of the lasting damage caused by brain drain. —Dave Mock, "3 Reasons to Be Bearish on IBM," *The Money Times*, April 18, 2009

Governor David A. Paterson today announced $280 million in grants to fund health care restructuring projects throughout New York State that will expand the availability of primary care in local communities, cut duplicative services in hospitals, "rightsize" nursing homes and fund consolidation projects by health care providers. —Rus Thompson, "Gov. Paterson Announces $280 Million in Grants," *Albany Insanity*, October 2, 2008

The obtuse response is to immediately rush in to rightsize the organization during downturns. —Adil Malia, "Don't Just Rush to the Treadmill," *The Wall Street Journal*, July 8, 2009

As workplaces continue to rightsize and downsize, we all find ourselves doing more with less. —"12 Ways to Boost Your Creativity at Work," *Ground Report*, January 14, 2009

One could say that *rightsize* is a euphemism of a euphemism, as *downsize* is a euphemism for "fire."

103 **risk management**
/ (risk man'ij-mənt)/

noun

- The process of determining the maximum acceptable level of overall risk to and from a proposed activity, then using risk assessment techniques to determine the initial level of risk and, if this is excessive, developing a strategy to ameliorate appropriate individual risks until the overall level of risk is reduced to an acceptable level.

Examples:

Since the risk management models used until now ignored the uncertainties inherent in reflexivity, limits on credit and leverage will have to be set substantially lower than those that were tolerated in the recent past. —George Soros, "The Crisis & What to Do About It," *The New York Review of Books*, December 4, 2008

At the same time, there can be valid policy reasons to allow risk management decisions to be influenced by sound scientific indications of danger that are yet not sufficiently well-established to qualify for inclusion into the scientific corpus. —"Risk," *Stanford Encyclopedia of Philosophy*, March 13, 2007

What will be needed then to keep a leash on this future Citigroup is a more well-educated regulator that truly understands the products and services Citigroup offers, and that employs real risk management professionals who can truly understand the risks associated with new initiatives. —"Citigroup Is Too Important to Fail, Which Is Why It's a Great Long Term Investment," *Seeking Alpha*, June 24, 2009

Risk management organizations determine specific *risk management* standards for companies to measure themselves against in different fields.

104 **rollout**

/ (rōl out)/

noun

- An act of rolling out or deployment.

Examples:

Apparently realizing that the Sarah Palin rollout is going badly, the GOP is holding a series of press conferences here in St. Paul to push back. —David Kurtz, "GOP: Battle Stations!" *TPM Election Central,* September 3, 2008

The new Pentagon budget rollout is part of a larger public relations campaign to promote a simple idea: We're no longer at war, but there's still plenty of fighting to do. —Ira Chernus, "Requiem for the War on Terror," *The Huffington Post,* April 9, 2009

Google's recommendation rollout is also a defensive move to maintain its dominance on the Web. —Laurie Burkitt, "The Race for Recommendations," *Forbes,* April 23, 2010

The rollout is all part of a redesigned USA.gov, the federal government's online home for services and information. — Ed O'Keefe, "Government launches new apps," *The Washington Post,* July 2, 2010

Rollout initially referred specifically to the introduction of new air-craft, but now refers to any new product or service.

105 scalable
/ (skāl'ə-bəl)/

adjective

1 Capable of being scaled.
2 Able to support the required quality of service as the system load increases.

Examples:
Our research shows that premium website solutions that are sold to [Home Owner Association] and similar organizations result in high registration rates, but are not typically scalable from a sales standpoint. —"Kansas City Tech Startup Neighbortree.com Launches Free Neighborhood Website Social Network," *Press Release Central*, July 27, 2010

"All our customers have a ton of development in scalable web-services based software platforms that they are trying to increase the scale of and reliability for—they are thinking hard about whether relational databases are the right underlying data management infrastructure," Wolski said. —Gavin Clarke, "Open sourcers pump Eucalyptus clouds with data," *The Register*, February 10, 2010

Nor should they spend a lot of time trimming our sails (as long as proposals remain "scalable") in the name of political expediency. —Merrill Goozner, "Shaping the Health Care Debate," *The Huffington Post*, January 29, 2007

This white paper examines how the Sun Oracle Exadata Storage Server allows companies to accelerate database performance, handle change and growth in scalable and incremental steps, and deliver mission-critical data availability and protection. —"Sun Oracle Exadata Storage Server and Database Machine," *BNET*, January 2009

Scalable is the adjective form of the verb *scale*, which comes from the Latin word *scālae*, meaning "ladder."

106 severance

/ (sev'ər-əns *or* sev'rəns)/

noun

- A payment given to employees whose jobs are eliminated, usually consisting of two weeks of pay for every year worked.

Examples:
Call me picky, but it also seems a stretch to call yourself a populist, as Fiorina has done every chance she gets, when you walked away from your last job with $21 million in

severance, have a yacht, a mansion, a condo in George-town, and have been able to funnel at least $5.5 million of your personal fortune into a Senate race. —Mona Gable, "Why Carly Fiorina Is Not Cool for California," *The Huffington Post*, June 6, 2010

For instance, the state may have to pay up to $40 million in severance to 2,600 employees and millions more to get out of contracts, including a $15 million trucking contract, according to sources in the governor's office. —Anita Kumar, "McDonnell wants to show Virginia the way out of liquor business," *The Washington Post*, July 18, 2010

He noted the [$12.2 million in] severance is a tiny fraction of the $125 billion HP expects to record in revenue this year. —Jordan Robertson, "Hurd reaps HP payday as investors suffer," *SF Gate*, August 9, 2010

Companies offer *severance payment* to employees who are *down-sized, laid off,* or *let go,* rather than *fired.* Employees are *fired* usually because of misconduct or poor performance.

107 **stakeholder**
/ (stāk'hōl,dər)/

noun

- A person or organization with a legitimate interest in a given situation, action, or enterprise.

Examples:

Indra Nooyi: So people are now beginning to embrace, faster than you'd ever imagine, that the stakeholder is the right person to focus on, because companies can do well, long term, only if the societies in which they operate also do well. —Kai Ryssdal, "PepsiCo CEO: Redefine profit and loss," *American Public Media*, January 29, 2010

But back at the workshop I was leading, the three dozen machers who came mainly from investment, technology, and education said something different: The stakeholder is taking control. —Jeff Jarvis, "Davos09: Starting Open Bank," *The Huffington Post*, February 1, 2009

Very few frauds result in SEC enforcement action; many more are adjudicated by class actions. Most are recorded only in stakeholder disappointment, large price drops, bond defaults and insolvency. —James A. Kaplan, "Why Corporate Fraud Is on the Rise," *Forbes*, June 10, 2010

An *internal stakeholder* is someone *within* the company who has a vested interest in the success of an endeavor.

strike

/ (strīk)/

verb

• To press a claim or demand by coercive or threatening action of some kind; in common usage, to quit work along with others, in order to compel an employer to accede to some demand, as for increase of pay, or to protest against something, as a reduction of wages: as, to strike for higher pay or shorter hours of work.

Examples:

What this strike is about is that writers—especially newer ones—have awakened to the reality that the studios are trying to corner us into a situation where we will ultimately get no residuals at all, simply by keeping the same contract we already have for the other transmission media, such as broadcast and cable, but not providing a decent rate when shows are broadcast originally or emanate from the network and are rerun over the Internet. —Michael Russnow, "The WGA Strike for Dummies, and My Concerns Over the DGA Deal," *The Huffington Post*, January 25, 2008

J. P. Morgan analyst Eric Selle said in a research report last week that he believes the strike is already eating away at GM's liquidity. —Terry Kosdrosky and Neal E. Boudette, "American Axle Strike Tests UAW Resolve," *The Wall Street Journal*, March 12, 2008

A *strike* is the opposite of a *lockout,* which is "a labor disruption where management refuses to allow workers into a plant to work even if they are willing."

109 synergy
/ (sin'ər-jē)/

noun
- Benefits resulting from combining two different groups, people, objects, or processes.

Examples:
"In order to gain synergy with the rest of the portfolio, Hindustan Coca-Cola Beverages (HCCBPL) has integrated the operations of some exclusive Kinley water franchise bottling partners in select territories in Tamil Nadu, Karnataka and Maharashtra with itself," a Coca-Cola India spokesperson told [Economic Times]. —"India News Digest: Boeing to Replicate U.S. Business Structure in India," *The Wall Street Journal*, August 9, 2009

The three branches of government must respect the limitations of their power and a way must be found for them to work in synergy or all the other ideas about priorities, betterment, etc. will remain futile. —Jennifer Bogut, "Here's My Take #2: The Top Three Issues for the Next Administration Are. . ." *The Huffington Post*, October 16, 2008

Synergy comes from the Greek word *sunergiā*, meaning "cooperation," and shouldn't be confused with *synergism*, "the theological doctrine that one's salvation is brought about by a combination of human will and divine grace."

110

throughput
/ (thrōō'poot)/

noun

1 The rate of production; the rate at which something can be processed.

2 The rate at which data is transferred through a system.

Examples:

If there are infinite reservoirs from which material can be obtained and into which effluvia can be deposited, then the throughput is at least a plausible measure of the success of the economy. —Kenneth Ewart Boulding, "The Economics of the Coming Spaceship Earth," *The Encyclopedia of Earth*, 1966

Even assuming that Nabucco's boosters manage to assemble a coterie of deep-pocketed suckers er, investors, the only promised current volume for Nabucco's proposed 31 billion cubic meters (bcm) annual throughput is Azerbaijan's future offshore Caspian Shah Deniz production, estimated at 8 bcm. —James Stafford, "The Myth of Nabucco: Greed, Delusion and $11.4 Billion," *OpEdNews.com*, January 5, 2010

Besides lower through-put with consumer demand flagging, customers could demand better pricing as piles of goods stack up at competitors that are either liquidating or in fear that they will be liquidated if they don't move as much inventory as possible. —Alan Brochstein, "Wal-Mart: Not So Safe Haven in a Challenging Economy," *Seeking Alpha*, January 18, 2009

Throughput and *bandwidth* are two terms from computing that are now often used in noncomputing contexts.

111

Total Quality Management
/ (tōt'l kwol'i-tē man'ij-mənt)/

noun
- A strategic approach to management aimed at embedding awareness of quality in all organizational processes.

Examples:
Improving central business processes is the core of most popular programs like continuous improvement, change

management, total quality management and others. —"Quick Guide: What is BPM?" *ebiz*, March 19, 2010

The balanced scorecard methodology, an outgrowth of prior measurement and management methodologies like total quality management (TQM), has existed for decades, but it was formalized in the early 1990s by Robert Kaplan and David Norton. —"Balanced Scorecard," *CIO.in*, April 11, 2009

Back in the 90s, when Total Quality Management was all the rage, business schools spent a lot of time digging up the post-WWII era work of Deming and Taguchi, which led to the quality programs at Toyota and other Japanese companies. —Sean Casten, "RPS, EERS and energy politics," *Grist*, April 9, 2009

In addition, Total Quality Management studies have shown that structured repeatable processes reduce errors and the requirements for rework, further reducing costs. —Daniel Magid, "Top Six Cost-Cutting Strategies for IT Compliance," *Sarbanes-Oxley Compliance Journal*, March 30, 2009

Mr. Butcher will continue the company's focus on Total Quality Management leading to accredited status in all properties while building a culture of innovation and continuous improvement. —"Langham Hotels International Appoints First CEO," *Hotel Interactive*, March 12, 2009

Total Quality Management (often abbreviated *TQM*) was coined by W. Edwards Deming, (1900–1993), an American statistician.

transparency

/ (trans-pâr'ən-sē *or* trans -par'ən-sē)/

noun
- The quality of being transparent; transparency, especially in regard to making public the reasons behind decision making or policy.

Examples:

This transparency is the peculiar mark of his greatness: he does not wish to puzzle or impress; he is not a virtuoso performer but a creator; his work is not a riddle to be solved but a realm to be explored. —Helen Muchnic, "Tolstoy the Great," *The New York Review of Books*, September 14, 1967

As a result, in an age when "transparency" is the business watchword, financial markets have become increasingly opaque. —Henry Kaufman, "Who's Watching the Big Banks?" *The Wall Street Journal*, November 13, 2007

Although I am not in a position to ascertain the sincerity of the president's oratory, his transparency is an unparalleled and long-needed improvement. —Nikolas D. Skalkotos, "Religion always seems to undermine peace," *Las Vegas Sun*, June 7, 2009

The value in transparency is giving people the power to be involved when they are able, not at a time of the government's choosing, i.e. common council meetings at 1PM on a Wednesday or non-indexed pdf's released after an endless series of FOIL requests. —Chris Smith, "Buffalo Crime Reports: Transparency," *WNY Media*, June 2, 2009

Businesses practice *transparency* by being open about their practices and decision-making processes.

113

turnaround
/ (tûrn'ə-round₁)/

noun
1 A reversal of policy.
2 The time required to carry out a task.

Examples:
We need fresh ideas because we are in a pivotal period. The numbers are getting worse rather than better. And, there are few indicators to suggest any sort of turn-around within the foreseeable future. —Ed Crego, George Munoz, and Frank Islam, "Converting Unemployment Benefits to Employment Benefits," *The Huffington Post*, August 3, 2010

IDT rang the NYSE opening bell on Monday, saying "After executing a successful turn-around, IDT has regained

compliance with the New York Stock Exchange's continued listing requirements and achieved bottom line profitability."
—"IDT in the Driver's Seat Wednesday," *Forbes*, June 30, 2010

This was Mr. Valenti's fifth hospital turn-around project, but his first with a public hospital. He says he did it by applying the "the private-practice business model" to the public hospital: he demanded individual accountability and financial accountability; he developed a clear strategic plan, and recruited people who could execute the plan; he changed the culture from one of inertia, defeat and pessimism, to one of excitement and belief in the future. —Abraham Verghese, MD, "Mending the Hospital Safety Net," *The Wall Street Journal*, August 7, 2009

A *turnaround specialist* is someone who is brought into a business to give it a new direction or to bring it back to profitability.

114 turnkey

/ (tûrn′kē͵)/

adjective
- Ready to use without further assembly or test; supplied in a state that is ready to turn on and operate (typically refers to an assembly that is outsourced for manufacture).

Examples:

Surprisingly, the old home was in "turnkey" condition—that is, except for the barn out back. —Johnny Williams, "Red Barn Renovation: Part 1–Where to Begin?" *Apartment Therapy*, November 30, 2009

Since 1996, Cendyn has excelled at being a full-service, interactive sales and marketing agency specializing in turnkey solutions for the hotel and travel industries. —"Palm Beach County CVB Partners with Cendyn for Online Campaigns That Fill Hotel Rooms, Attract Visitors to Area Businesses," *PR Web*, July 22, 2010

The Wholesale Plans Division specializes in turnkey, private label membership benefit plans offered through retail outlets including rent-to-own centers. —"Alliance HealthCard, Inc. Changes Corporate Name to Access Plans, Inc.; Stock Symbol to Change," *Market Wire*, December 7, 2009

Turnkey's original meaning was "a warder or jailer, a keeper of the keys in a prison."

115 **turnover**

/ (tûrn'ō,vər)/

noun

1 The amount of a material that is turned over, or on which some process is carried out: nearly equivalent to *output*.

2 The amount of money turned over or drawn in a business, as in a retail shop, in a specified time.

3 The number of employees or customers who leave a business in a specified time.

Examples:

Added value, such as the new super-ATM, creates excellent public relations, reduces customer turn-over, and increases consumer loyalty. —Jim Luce, "Goodbye, Western Union? Overseas Remittances Now ATM to ATM," *The Huffington Post*, March 15, 2010

But because of the slow turn-over of the overall fleet, gasoline consumption would be reduced only modestly below what it would otherwise be. —Daniel Yergin, "Why Oil Still Has a Future," *The Wall Street Journal*, August 30, 2009

Korea has perhaps the world's highest political turn-over rate. A very high percentage of incumbents are voted out of office regularly in local, provincial and national elections. In the 2004 parliamentary elections, for example, only one third of those elected to the National Assembly were incumbents—the lowest number in recent memory, say experts. —"Incumbents, Beware," *Newsweek*, June 5, 2006

Turnover is sometimes written as turnover rate.

116

upstream

/ (up strēm)/

adjective or adverb

- In a direction against the flow of a current or stream; up-river; in business, closer to exploration and preproduction than to refining and selling.

Examples:

The Yangtze River carves a deep course through this part of China (it's a few hundred miles upstream from the Three Gorges region), and high-rises are arrayed on the hillsides, plateaus and valleys. —Daniel Gross, "Hot Pot's Top Spot," *Newsweek*, November 20, 2009

Sport fishermen had complained for years that oil production in upstream Arkansas was spewing thousands of gallons of salty water into the watershed, making the creek inhospitable to fish. —Emma Brown, "Murray Stein, advocate for clean waterways, dies at 92," *The Washington Post*, June 7, 2010

"Downstream results are a bit better, upstream is in line and financials are better," Banesto analyst Robert Jackson said. —Bernd Radowitzh, "Repsol Swings to Loss on Falling Oil," *The Wall Street Journal*, February 27, 2009

At a UN high-level event on food security, World Bank managing director Ngozi Okonjo-Iweala spoke eloquently about the unique need for the initiative to carefully consider girls in upstream design to ensure they are part of the solution. —Maria Eitel, "At CGI and Beyond, World Leaders Say Girls Are the Key to Progress," *The Huffington Post*, September 30, 2009

In computing, *upstream* can mean in the direction from the client to the server.

use case

/ (yōōz kās)/

noun
- A description of a potential scenario in which a system receives an external request (such as user input) and responds to it. Also written *use-case*.

Examples:
The use case in these countries is radically different from Western Europe, the U.S. and Canada. —Anton Denissov, "What's Lighting the Fire Under Mobile Broadband?" *E-Commerce Times*, January 2, 2009

When you think about the original use case of Twitter, which @Leisa described so wonderfully as "ambient intimacy," it's really news from your close friends. But it's news nonetheless. —Tim O'Reilly, "My 140conf Talk: Twitter as Publishing," *O'Reilly Radar*, June 24, 2009

It was then rolled out to other destinations and multiple segments to track a wide variety of oil field equipment ranging from sophisticated electronic isolation valves to simple metal containers and baskets with each type of asset having its own use-case and process life-cycle. —"RFID Asset Tracking Solutions Provider AssetPulse Completes International Deployments for the Oil and Gas Industry," *PR Web*, August 14, 2010

What the industry needed was an objective set of ideas for how mashups could add value, regardless of the particular tool. I realized that a lot of my thoughts could be distilled into generic patterns. Not quite the academic, Gang-of-Four kind, but something a little more rooted in practical use cases. —John Musser, "Enterprise Mashups: New Book Highlights Patterns," *Programmable Web*, January 7, 2009

Use case is a term often used in software engineering.

value-add

118

/ (val'yoo ad)/

noun

- Something that adds value; a benefit or enhancement.

Examples:

"It's a tremendous value-add—one more thing to help attract customers to our broadband service," says spokesman
Cliff Lee, who adds that Verizon has also bought into Dis-
ney's and the NFL's paid offerings. —Eliot Von Buskirk, "ESPN
to ISPs: Pay for Your Customers to Play Video," *Wired*, February 5, 2009

It is conceivable that all of the transactional elements within a branch will be moved to automated banking within
electronic banking centres, automated branches, ATMs or
the Internet within the next 5-10 years. What then is left?
The face-to-face, value-add of a real, live human interaction. —Brett King, "What the Bank Branch Will Become," *The Huffington Post*, June 30, 2010

As 4G wireless networks and IPv6 roll out, the value-add to
customers of NetLogic's chip families improves, thus ben-
efiting unit volumes, average selling price and margins, as
both wireline and wireless operators are forced into wholesale capacity modernization. —Rick Whittington, "Analog Chips
Drive the Industrial Boom," *Forbes*, June 8, 2010

Value-add is not to be confused with *value-added*, which is the estimated value added to a product at each stage of its production or
distribution. *Value-added tax (VAT)* is "a tax levied on the difference
between a commodity's price before taxes and its cost of production."

119 win-win

/ (win win)/

adjective
- Of a situation or outcome that benefits two parties, or that has two distinct benefits.

Examples:
Team with a professor at your local university. . . . If a professor does the application with you and gets to publish the results, that's a win-win situation. —Martin Zilling, "Top 10 Sources of Funding for Start-Ups," *Forbes*, February 12, 2010

That's curious considering that reducing America's oil imports while investing in renewable energy to cut back the nation's carbon emissions used to be almost a no-brainer, even a win-win (after cap-and-trade was deemed all but dead in the Senate earlier this year). —Daniel Stone, "After Banking Reform, Energy Still Sits on Ice," *Newsweek*, April 27, 2010

"It is a win-win situation for both companies as Videocon, with a low cost base and large manufacturing facilities, gets access to a global brand," said Alok Shende, principal analyst and founder director of Ascentius, a technology research firm. —Kenan Machado, "Videocon to Make, Sell Philips' TV Sets in India," *The Wall Street Journal*, April 19, 2010

Win-win is a type of negotiation, or "the process of achieving agreement through discussion."

work-flow or workflow

/ (wûrk′flō‚)/

noun

1 The rate at which a flow of work takes place.
2 The process and/or procedure by which tasks are completed.

Examples:

One big reason digital newsrooms seem so foreign and stressful to those who have spent their careers in print is that the digital product, production schedules, goals, work-flow, reporting styles, and skill-sets are so different. —Henry Blodget, "Some Thoughts on Digital Media and the Future of the Newspaper Business," *The Huffington Post*, July 21, 2010

"I have those deadlines tattooed on my forehead," says Transportation Secretary Norman Mineta, sitting beside a huge, finely detailed milestone and work-flow chart that he keeps next to his conference table. —"This Dog Won't Hurt," *Newsweek*, June 3, 2002

Yet web-mail is also important because such mail applications usually tend to occupy a significant place in the work-flow for most people, and the more this moves out of the realm of dedicated desktop devices, the more that it diminishes people's use of other non-desktop systems in favor of browser oriented ones. —Kurt Cagle, "Analysis 2009: Application services come into their own," *O'Reilly Community*, January 6, 2009

Workflow may be shown with a flowchart, which defines actors, actions, results, decisions, and action paths.